RAND

An Inventory of Transport Safety Information in the Netherlands

James P. Kahan, John A. Stoop,
Lisa van Dorp, Erik J. Frinking,
Etienne M. van der Horst,
Kerry M. Malone

Supported by the
Netherlands Ministry of Transport,
Public Works and Water Management

European-American Center for Policy Analysis

Preface

This report, prepared for the Project Realisatie Transportongevallenraad of the Ministerie van Verkeer en Waterstaat, the Netherlands, presents an inventory of information regarding transport safety information that was available in the Netherlands at the end of 1995. The inventory is focused on the registration and recording of transport accidents and incidents in air, rail, road, inland waterway, and maritime transport. It is organized in two separate ways: by organization processing the information and by database. The report should be of interest to persons concerned with transport safety and with information processing for public policy making.

An Inventory of Transport Safety Information in the Netherlands was prepared by the European-American Center for Policy Analysis (EAC), a unit of RAND. The EAC was assisted by the faculty of Systems Engineering, Policy Analysis, and Management (SEPA) at the Technological University of Delft. The Director of RAND/EAC is Richard Fallon. Communications regarding this report may be addressed to him:

Richard Fallon, Ph.D.
EAC
Landbergstraat 6
2628 CE Delft
The Netherlands
Telephone: +31–15–278.54.11
Fax: +31–15–278.17.88

Contents

Summary

The Netherlands will establish a unified national transportation safety board, or Transportongevallenraad (TOR — translated into English as Transport Safety Board), which should be fully functional by mid-1997. The board will be responsible for air, sea, inland waterway, railroad, and road transport, as outlined in the draft enabling legislation *Concept Transportongevallenwet*, and it will have two primary objectives:

- to conduct independent investigations of transport accidents and incidents[1] (collectively called *events*), and

- to recommend ways of mitigating and eliminating threats to safety.

The establishment of the TOR is a major policy change for the Netherlands; the investigative function of five separate bodies dealing with air, rail, road, maritime shipping, and inland shipping will be incorporated into the new board that examines transport safety as a whole instead of by modality.

The Ministerie van Verkeer en Waterstaat has created a "Project Realisatie Transportongevallenraad" (PRT) to implement the TOR. Among the tasks of the PRT are the following:

- to determine the structure, composition, and rules of procedure of the TOR, in accordance with the board's mission and responsibilities. While some aspects of the TOR are well-defined by law, many others require attention.

- to establish an information structure for the TOR. The board will have its own professional expertise and the power to hold hearings, obtain data, and contract for research. In order to manage these diverse sources of information, it must (1) understand what information is available from what sources and (2) be able to integrate information from these diverse sources.

To assist it in performing its mission, the PRT asked RAND/EAC for support in the form of policy research. The present document, the first part of that support, is an inventory of current information available in the Netherlands that could be used by the TOR in fulfilling its missions.

---

[1]An incident is an event that "but for the grace of God" would have been an accident. More formally, it is defined in the *Concept Transportongevallenwet* as an event related to the use of transport that is not an accident, in which the safety of third parties or passengers was actually endangered.

The inventory was taken by the EAC between late October and mid-December 1995, using a series of face-to-face interviews and telephone conversations with members of organizations identified as producing or using information about transport safety. Appendix B lists the organizations and individuals contacted. Because of time constraints, it was not possible to verify the quality of the information other than through personal recommendations, published documents, and other written materials provided by the interviewees.

Organizations Contacted

The EAC contacted 26 different organizations or types of organizations. This report describes each organization in sentence-outline form, giving (A) the mode(s) of transport examined, (B) the missions of the organization as they relate to the TOR, (C) the sources of information of these organizations, (D) how the organizations process information, and (E) where and how these organizations disseminate their findings with regard to transport safety. The 26 organizations, which are listed below, include the five Dutch boards concerned with transport safety plus governmental inspectorates and data-gathering agencies, primary data collectors, and selected research organizations.

1. Raad voor de Luchtvaart (RVL)

2. Spoorwegongevallenraad (SOR)

3. Raad voor de Scheepvaart (RVS)

4. Commissie Binnenvaart Rampenwet (CBR)

5. Raad voor de Verkeersveiligheid (RVV)

6. Rijksluchtvaartdienst-Luchtvaartinspectie (RLD-LI)

7. Air Traffic Incident Commission (ATIC)

8. Nationaal Lucht-en Ruimtevaart Laboratorium (NLR)

9. Railned

10. Directoraat-Generaal Scheepvaart en Maritieme Zaken-Scheepvaartinspectie (DGSM-SI)

11. Permanente Kontactgroep Opsporing Noordzee (PKON)

12. Maritiem Simulatie Centrum Nederland (MSCN)

13. Shipping insurers

14. Adviesdienst Verkeer en Vervoer-Afdeling Leefbaarheid (AVV-VLL)

15. Korps Landelijke Politiediensten (KLPD)

16. Rijksdienst voor het Wegverkeer (RDW)

17. Stichting Wetenschappelijk Onderzoek Verkeersveiligheid (SWOV)

18. TNO-Wegtransportmiddelen (TNO-WT)

19. TNO-Technische Menskunde (TNO-TM)

20. TNO-Preventie & Gezondheid (TNO-P&G)

21. Automobile insurers

22. Adviesdienst Verkeer en Vervoer-Afdeling Basisgegevens (AVV-BG)

23. Rijksverkeersinspectie (RVI)

24. Commissie Transport Gevaarlijke Goederen (CTGG)

25. TNO-Industriële Veiligheid (TNO-IV)

26. University research groups

Information Streams Examined

The study began with the examination of 22 different streams of information, tracing them from inception through dissemination and use. Not included in this inventory were the hearings and qualitative investigations conducted by the five existing modal boards.

To facilitate comparisons, each information stream was organized according to a common format: (A) the mode(s) of transport examined, (B) the primary sources of information for the stream, (C) the processing performed on the information by each organization that handled the stream, (D) the utility of the information for the TOR, and (E) various quality characteristics of the information, such as its validity, independence of collection and processing, freedom from bias, and availability.

The 22 information streams investigated were the following:

1. RVL investigations

2. RLD-LI inspections

3. the ATIC database

4. the OASIS (Operational Airport Safety Information System) database

5. the NLR air movements database

6. the NLR air accidents database

7. MISOS (Management Informatie Systeem Ongevallen)

8. the RVI rail accident database

9. the NEVLOG (the registry of vessels maintained by the DGSM-SI)

10. the NEBAG (the personnel [captains, pilots, etc.] registry of the DGSM-SI)

11. the ORS (Ongevallen Registratie Systeem), the SI (Scheepvaart Inspectie) Ongevallen database, and the ONOVIS (the relational database of water transport accidents being constructed by DGSM-SI and AVV-BG)

12. MSCN models

13. Shipping insurers' databases

14. the Wegongevallen database

15. Road insurers' investigations

16. RVI inspections

17. RDW vehicle roadworthiness certifications

18. APK and RDW inspections

19. RDW bus accident investigations

20. the VIPORS (Verkeersincidenten en Privéongevallen Registratie Systeem)

21. CTGG information on hazardous materials

22. the TNO-IV FACTS database on worldwide hazardous materials accidents

At the end of this inventory of information streams are other information streams that might be useful to the TOR.

Emerging Issues

In the course of the examination, several aspects of information flow regarding transport safety emerged as important considerations for the TOR.

Investigations versus Research. It is useful to distinguish between the terms "investigation" and "research." The critical distinction is whether the focus is on a single event or on multiple events. An *investigation* is an in-depth empirical study of a single event, looking at the available data from as many different aspects as possible in order to understand as thoroughly as possible that event. A *research study*, on the other hand, is an empirical examination of events that attempts, by using analytic tools of data reduction, to sort out commonalities and differences among the events and the factors that determine such commonalities and differences.

Both investigation and research are called for in the TOR's mandate. Investigation is an expressed function, while research is implied by the need to make safety recommendations. While the value of research seems obvious, it is important to remember that the association between research and governmental functions has historically not been uniformly rewarding. Any TOR use of research must therefore produce visible and significant benefits.

The problem of denominators. An inherent part of safety assessment is determining the risk of accident, if not in precise numerical terms, then at least in rough verbal terms. An ongoing problem in such assessments is that, while the incidence of specific hazards (e.g., road fatalities, train derailments) may be well-known, the body of events that might have become accidents but did not is unknown. In other words, in accident analyses, investigations can often provide information about numerators but rarely about denominators. Research is needed to reduce data from various sources into reasonable denominators.

Intended versus real uses of information. Information gathered with one purpose in mind can often be successfully employed for other purposes. However, even when data are carefully and objectively gathered, they may be biased if the context is changed. For the TOR, this issue is important because all Dutch investigative and research bodies depend heavily on police reports of accidents. The potential discrepancy between the needs of policy departments and the needs of the TOR can lead to less-than-desirable data collection and therefore incomplete or incorrect conclusions, even when the independence of the transport safety board is guaranteed.

The limitations of single-modality approaches. Limitations to single-modality approaches result, for a number of reasons, in incomplete pictures of transport safety. Interactions between modalities (e.g., rail lines that cross roads or the act of transferring cargo from ship to truck) can fall outside the responsibility of single modalities. Lessons available from one modality (e.g., in human factors) may not be learned from another. Multimodality approaches, including a unified investigative staff for the TOR, will lessen these limitations.

Conclusion

This inventory of Dutch information regarding transport safety covers all of the obvious information streams and touches upon some of the less-obvious ones. It represents a wealth of information that could illuminate our understanding of the causes of accidents, both in general and specifically. Much of this information is currently used, but a fair amount has not yet been tapped.

There are great differences among and within transport modalities in availability of information, comprehensiveness of data, and freedom of the data collection process from bias. Some of these differences are inherent in the nature of the type of information sought, but others are due more to organizations' standard operating procedures. A fresh look at these practices might have beneficial results.

In compiling this inventory of information about transport safety, a number of issues relating to the informational and organizational structure of the TOR arose, including: the need to distinguish between investigation and research and to use both in synthesis, the need to detect causal patterns in accidents, the problem of incomplete denominators in analyses of risk, biases that may result when information collected for one purpose is used for another, and the inherent limitations of restricting one's view of transport safety to one modality at a time. A study of each of these issues would benefit the performance of the TOR.

Acknowledgments

We would like to thank the persons and organizations listed in Appendix B for their time and cooperative spirit in providing us with the information needed to compile this inventory. Mw. C. Groenendijk greatly assisted us by keeping track of appointments and managing the correspondence of the project. We benefited from critical readings of earlier drafts of the manuscript by ir. I. F. H. C. C. van den Enden, prof. dr. ir. R. E. C. M. van der Heijden, and prof. dr. ir. J. L. de Kroes.

1. Introduction

Background

On 28 March 1995, the Tweede Kamer der Staten-Generaal passed a motion regarding the establishment of a unified national transportation safety board ("Instelling van een Raad voor de transportveiligheid").[2] This motion concluded debate and discussion that had taken place over the previous two years regarding the needs of the Dutch with respect to monitoring, investigating, and preventing accidents arising from all modes of transport and the need for a board to advise the Ministerie van Verkeer en Waterstaat (V&W) on appropriate transportation safety policy. Specifics regarding the establishment of the Transport Safety Board (Transportongevallenraad, henceforth abbreviated TOR), which is responsible for air, sea, inland waterway, railroad, and road transport, have been set out in the *Concept Transportongevallenwet*.[3] It is planned that the TOR will be fully functional by mid-1997.

The TOR will have two primary functions:

- conducting independent investigations of transport accidents and incidents[4] (collectively called *events*), and

- recommending ways of mitigating and eliminating threats to safety.

In order to fulfill these functions, the TOR must be able to *initiate major examinations* of safety problems by investigating individual events and possibly other triggering situations, *determine the major causal factors* leading to events, and *identify changes* to transport practices that will reduce the likelihood or effect of events. This implies that the TOR must also have the functions of:

- monitoring transport safety and the factors influencing it, and

- identifying problem situations.

---

[2]Tweede Kamer der Staten-Generaal Vergaderjaar 1994-1995, 23674.

[3]The most recent version of this document is dated 19 February 1996.

[4]An incident is an event that "but for the grace of God" would have been an accident. More formally, it is defined in the *Concept Transportongevallenwet* as an event related to the use of transport that was not an accident—in which the safety of third parties or passengers was actually endangered.

The establishment of the TOR is a major policy change for the Netherlands. Up until now, separate bodies have had responsibility for the different transportation modes. This separation existed because it was believed that safety investigations had to take place within the independently developed traditions, working methods, compositions, and missions of the different modes. Thus, four bodies investigate transport accidents:

- the Raad voor de Luchtvaart (RVL) for air,
- the Spoorwegongevallenraad (SOR) for rail,
- the Commissie Binnenvaart Rampenwet (CBR) for inland waterways, and
- the Raad voor de Scheepvaart (RVS) for sea.

In addition, the Raad voor de Verkeersveiligheid (RVV), an advisory body regarding road transport safety, can, if it chooses, initiate an investigation of road accidents.

The Netherlands is one of the pioneers in the establishment of independent bodies responsible for transportation safety. It is also founder of the International Transportation Safety Association ITSA (full membership in ITSA requires that a nation have independent transportation safety boards).[5] Among ITSA nations, however, there is a strong movement toward unified boards. The United States was the first to unify transportation safety, with the establishment of the National Transportation Safety Board in 1977. Canada and Sweden followed suit in 1990, New Zealand in 1992, and Finland's unified board began officially functioning on 1 March 1996.

The V&W has created a Project Realisatie Transportongevallenraad (PRT) to implement the TOR. Among the tasks of the PRT are the following:

- determining the structure, composition, and rules of procedure of the TOR, in accordance with the mission and responsibilities as given by the Tweede Kamer and V&W. While some aspects of the TOR are well-defined, there are many others that require attention.

- determining an information structure for the TOR. The board will have its own expertise. It will also have the power to hold hearings, obtain data, and contract for research. In order to manage these diverse sources of information, the board must (1) understand what information is available from what sources and (2) know how to integrate information from these diverse sources.

- managing the transition from the current situation of multiple boards to the establishment of the TOR. There will be both gaps and overlaps in responsibilities, personnel, and investigations in the transition period, which will occur largely during the second half of 1996.

---

[5]As of this writing, the full members of ITSA are Canada, Finland, the Netherlands, New Zealand, Russia, Sweden, and the United States of America.

To assist it in performing its mission, the PRT asked the RAND/European-American Center for Policy Analysis (EAC) for support in the form of policy research. The present document, the first part of that support, is an inventory of information available in the Netherlands that could be used by the TOR in fulfilling its missions. As such, it presents the results of Task 1A in the contract between the EAC and the V&W:

> The study of transport safety and investigation of transport accidents and incidents in the Netherlands is presently dispersed over governmental agencies, university faculties, and public and private research organizations. Different bodies examine different problems at different levels of detail, with different data, different analytic capabilities, and different objectives. There is no single repository of information, much less a capability of integrating information. Our first task, therefore, is to bring coherence to the picture of safety research on a national level in the Netherlands, by surveying what is being done and organizing the results of that survey into a taxonomy that will inform the needs assessment and functional assessment that follow.

To perform this task, the EAC conducted, between late October and mid-December 1995, a series of face-to-face interviews and telephone conversations with members of organizations identified as producing or using information about transport safety.[6] The short time period available meant that completeness of this inventory could not be guaranteed: some organizations on the contact list could not be interviewed in the time span allotted, while others were discovered too late to try to make appointments. Among the potentially important institutes and organizations that were not examined are the following:

- Alarmcentrale ANWB
- Amsterdam Airport Schiphol
- Centrale Post Ambulancevervoer
- Gemeentelijk Havenbedrijf Rotterdam
- KLM
- Koninklijke Nederlandse Reddings Maatschappij
- Loodswezen
- Radio Medische Dienst van het Rode Kruis
- Spoorwegtoezicht

Moreover, it was not possible to make first-hand assessments of the quality of the information. The EAC relied on what was related, backed up in many instances by published documents and other written materials provided by the interviewees.

_____

[6]Although this report is written in English, all interviews and telephone calls were conducted in Dutch.

Outline of This Paper

Section 1 of this report presents background information on the project. The next two sections present the inventory in two different ways: Section 2 presents the organizations that are involved with transport safety, presenting the different forms of information that are used by each organization. The following 26 organizations or types of organizations are discussed:

1. Raad voor de Luchtvaart (RVL)

2. Spoorwegongevallenraad (SOR)

3. Raad voor de Scheepvaart (RVS)

4. Commissie Binnenvaart Rampenwet (CBR)

5. Raad voor de Verkeersveiligheid (RVV)

6. Rijksluchtvaartdienst-Luchtvaartinspectie (RLD-LI)

7. Air Traffic Incident Commission (ATIC)

8. Nationaal Lucht-en Ruimtevaart Laboratorium (NLR)

9. Railned

10. Directoraat-Generaal Scheepvaart en Maritieme Zaken-Scheepvaartinspectie (DGSM-SI)

11. Permanente Kontactgroep Opsporing Noordzee (PKON)

12. Maritiem Simulatie Centrum Nederland (MSCN)

13. Shipping insurers

14. Adviesdienst Verkeer en Vervoer-Afdeling Leefbaarheid (AVV-VLL)

15. Korps Landelijke Politiediensten (KLPD)

16. Rijksdienst voor het Wegverkeer (RDW)

17. Stichting Wetenschappelijk Onderzoek Verkeersveiligheid (SWOV)

18. TNO-Wegtransportmiddelen (TNO-WT)

19. TNO-Technische Menskunde (TNO-TM)

20. TNO-Preventie & Gezondheid (TNO-P&G)

21. Automobile insurers

22. Adviesdienst Verkeer en Vervoer-Afdeling Basisgegevens (AVV-BG)

23. Rijksverkeersinspectie (RVI)

24. Commissie Transport Gevaarlijke Goederen (CTGG)

25. TNO-Industriële Veiligheid (TNO-IV)

26. University research groups

Section 3 presents each stream of information, which may encounter several organizations as it flows from source to use. Rudimentary assessments of the information are made in terms of its history, availability on electronic media, independence of source, and freedom from bias. The following 21 such streams are discussed:

1. RVL investigations

2. RLD-LI inspections

3. ATIC database

4. OASIS database

5. NLR Air Movements Database

6. NLR Air Accidents Database

7. MISOS

8. RVI rail accident database

9. NEVLOG registry of vessels

10. NEBAG Personnel (Captains, Pilots, etc.) Registry

11. ORS (Ongevallen Registratie Systeem), the SI Ongevallen database, and ONOVIS

12. MSCN models

13. Shipping insurers databases

14. Wegongevallen database

15. Road insurers investigations

16. RVI inspections

17. RDW vehicle roadworthiness certification

18. APK and RDW inspections

19. RDW bus accident investigations

20. Verkeersincidenten en Privéongevallen Registratie Systeem (VIPORS)

21. CTGG information on hazardous materials

22. TNO-IV FACTS database

Section 4 briefly discusses some general observations.

Finally, Appendix A provides a glossary of all acronyms used in this report, Appendix B lists in tabular form the organizations and people we contacted for this inventory, while Appendix C presents published documents that were reviewed.

2. Organizations

For ease of comparison, the organizations are categorized according to a common format. After giving the name and brief description the following is presented in sentence-outline form:

A.. Mode(s) of transport examined

B. Missions of the organization (related to TOR missions)

C. Sources of information

D. Processing of information

E. Dissemination of information

The inventory begins with the five national boards concerned with transport safety. It continues by presenting the organizations by modality: air, rail, water, road, and, finally, combined. Within each modality, governmental inspectorates and data-gathering functions are covered first, followed by primary data collectors, and concluding with research organizations.

National Boards and Commissions

1. Raad voor de Luchtvaart (RVL). The RVL is responsible for investigating all accidents and incidents regarding air both in the Netherlands and outside the country if a Dutch carrier or a Dutch-manufactured aircraft is involved. Each year, it investigates 28-35 accidents and about 120 incidents considered serious enough to investigate.

A. **Mode.** Air

B. **Mission.** The mission of the RVL is to investigate the causes of air accidents and incidents. This mission will be subsumed as part of the air *kamer*[7] under the TOR.[8]

C. **Sources.** The RVL has a small investigative body of its own. Most of its information comes from other sources, including the RLD (Rijksluchtvaartdienst), airline companies, aircraft manufacturers, flight and

---

[7]The TOR will have separate *kamers* (Dutch for "chambers") for air, rail, water, and road transport.

[8]The RVL only fulfills the investigatory role of the TOR, not the role of monitoring safety and the factors that influence it. Therefore, there cannot be a direct transfer of information structure from the RVL to the TOR.

cockpit recorders, and the ATIC (Air Traffic Incident Commission). For accidents, the information stream is as complete as possible, while for incidents, only those deemed serious by the sender are received by RVL, and only some of these are investigated.

D. **Processing.** RVL processing of accident and incident information follows international conventions, as set down by the International Civil Aviation Organization (ICAO) Annex 13. However, the RVL's own internal procedures for investigation are more stringent than those of ICAO. When other nations are involved (e.g., a foreign carrier in a Dutch accident or a Dutch carrier abroad), the RVL attempts to work together with its corresponding foreign body.

E. **Dissemination.** The RVL's end product of an accident investigation is a public report, which is sent to the V&W. If the report contains a recommendation, the minister must respond to that recommendation within one year. Investigations of incidents are also available, but no effort is made to make the public more aware of them. The RVL does not publish an annual summary, nor does it have its own databases of accidents and major incidents.

2. **Spoorwegongevallenraad (SOR).** The SOR can trace its inception to 1915 and its present form to 1956, making it a well-established institution. It is responsible for monitoring all matters that might affect the safety of the rail system. In practice, the SOR investigates all major rail accidents in the Netherlands[9] and can on its own initiative investigations into incidents or other situations bearing on rail safety that come to its attention. It generally does not investigate accidents in other countries, even if Dutch rolling stock is involved.

A. **Mode.** Rail, including trains and metro, but not trams, sneltrams, or developing systems such as peoplemovers.

B. **Mission.** The mission of the SOR is the same for rail as is that of the TOR for all transport modes. The SOR will be incorporated into the TOR.

C. **Sources.** For the most part, the SOR relies on information provided to it by Railned (see below). SOR members may direct investigations at accident sites. The SOR has a limited information-gathering capacity of its own supported by a small databank. It can hold hearings similar to those held by the RVL.

D. **Processing.** The SOR examines information to determine the causes of accidents and to identify characteristics of the rail system that are unsafe and need correction. This is an informal process that relies on the expertise of SOR staff.

---

[9]A major, or Class I, accident involves fatalities, material damages exceeding 5 million guilders, or a very high public profile.

E. Dissemination. SOR recommendations are publicly available. The institution has only just begun to issue annual reports.

3. Raad voor de Scheepvaart (RVS). The RVS has its origin in the Schepenwet (maritime law) of 1909. It is responsible for investigating the causes of maritime incidents and accidents anywhere in the world that involve Dutch maritime vessels or Dutch-licensed maritime personnel. Each year, the RVS investigates about 40 of the 120-130 maritime accidents registered by the DGSM-SI (Directoraat-Generaal Scheepvaart en Maritieme Zaken-Scheepvaartinspectie). In these investigations, the RVS holds hearings and issues findings. Through the instrument of the *tuchtrechtspraak*, it can issue disciplinary sanctions against responsible Dutch-licensed personnel for violating safe maritime practice.[10]

A. Mode. Sea

B. Mission. The mission of the RVS is to investigate accidents and incidents involving Dutch seagoing vessels. Except for the *tuchtrechtspraak*, it will be subsumed under the TOR.

C. Sources. The primary source of information for the RVS is reports of preliminary investigations given to it by the DGSM-SI, Afdeling Onderzoek en Ongevallen, which in turn are largely based on police reports. RVS members may look at accident sites, but the Raad has no information-gathering capacity of its own, other than the testimony in it obtains during hearings.

D. Processing. The RVS holds public hearings on cases it selects on the basis of DGSM-SI reports, taking testimony from interested parties and other witnesses. It then issues a verdict on the cause of the event. If the cause involves culpability (unsafe seamanship), the RVS can suspend (for a maximum of two years) the license of the guilty party.

E. Dissemination. The RVS publishes each of its verdicts as an appendix to the Staatscourant. Reprints are available upon request.

4. Commissie Binnenvaart Rampenwet (CBR). The CBR was established to investigate inland shipping accidents of all sorts. It does not have any specific responsibilities and can choose what to investigate. The CBR's concern is with the legal and economic aspects of accidents as well as the human costs. Its domain includes any accident occurring on Dutch inland waters, but not Dutch inland craft in foreign waters.

A. Mode. Inland waterways

---

[10] This disciplinary function is unique among transport safety bodies in the Netherlands. Such a function is not part of the TOR mandate and will not be subsumed under the TOR.

B. **Mission.** To investigate accidents and incidents involving inland shipping. This mission will be subsumed under the TOR.

C. **Sources.** The primary information source is the DGSM-SI, which passes on preliminary findings, based almost always on police reports. In addition, the CBR can hold hearings.

D. **Processing.** Expert judgment by the members of the commissie on what caused the accident.

E. **Dissemination.** CBR reports are published in the Staatscourant.

5. **Raad voor de Verkeersveiligheid (RVV).** The RVV was formally installed in 1981 as an advisory board for the several ministries responsible for transport safety. It is concerned with road transport, including vehicles, road infrastructure, drivers, and traffic control and monitoring policy. The purpose of the RVV is to make policy recommendations, either upon its own initiative or upon request from a ministry or parliament. Informally, it also helps set the political and public agenda for road safety matters. In the process of coming to a recommendation, the RVV is empowered to gather information by commissioning studies and holding hearings.

A. **Mode.** Road

B. **Mission.** Although the nominal objective of the RVV is to offer policy recommendations, while the TOR is explicitly not an advisory council, the RVV has acted as the major Dutch board concerned with road safety. The RVV has generally not been an investigatory body; only twice has it commissioned full-scale investigations of major events. However, many of its recommendations have focused on ways of mitigating and eliminating threats to safety. The RVV will be dissolved no later than January 1998; its policy mission will be absorbed by the Raad voor Verkeer en Waterstaat (RVW) and its safety oversight mission by the TOR.

C. **Sources.** The RVV's sources of information are specific to the task that it accepts or sets for itself. It can, and has, used independent investigations by commissioned experts, analyses from governmental and other research institutes, and testimony from expert and observer witnesses.

D. **Processing.** The RVV does no formal analyses of its own but rather integrates information provided to it.

E. **Dissemination.** RVV recommendations are published and available to the public. Although reaction to its recommendations is not mandatory, such is usually forthcoming. The RVV publishes an annual summary of its activities.

Air

6. Rijksluchtvaartdienst-Luchtvaartinspectie (RLD-LI). The RLD-LI is the branch of the RLD that monitors aircraft inspections and the civil aviation infrastructure in the Netherlands.[11] Its inspection function examines technical and managerial aspects of aviation, and it oversees the air traffic control organization (the LVB). Up until 1993, it was also charged with investigating accidents, but the RVL has assumed that responsibility. The RLD-LI has a voice in policy aspects of aviation, especially when they concern safety.

A. **Mode.** Air

B. **Mission.** The main task of the RLD-LI is to oversee all technical aspects regarding the safety and good functioning of the Dutch aviation infrastructure, which includes airports, air traffic control, airframe manufacturers, and air carriers. It also serves as the Dutch member of international aviation safety bodies.

C. **Sources.** The RLD-LI has a staff of 160, most of whom are involved in the inspection of the civil aviation infrastructure. For aircraft, RLD-LI relies on air carriers and airframe manufacturers to carry out their own inspections and report the results. All inspection, standardization, and maintenance data are reported only on paper. Additional information is obtained from the air industry, the NLR (Nationaal Lucht-en Ruimtevaart Laboratorium), university and other research organizations, the Dutch air force, and air traffic controllers, as needed.

D. **Processing.** Processing of information follows international (ICAO, JAA [Joint Aviation Authorities]) standards. The RLD-LI does not have the capability to examine aircraft, carriers, etc. to identify safety-related trends, but instead relies on the ICAO for internationally generated databases and results. As a participant in international groups, the RLD-LI has a role in commissioning safety studies and evaluating data. Because the JAA has its headquarters in Hoofddorp, the RLD-LI has a role and importance in that organization beyond that which would be due a country the size of the Netherlands.

E. **Dissemination.** RLD-LI information contains proprietary data and therefore is generally not publicly available. Both RLD-LI and international reports, stripped of any information that might identify sources, are publicly available.

7. Air Traffic Incident Commission (ATIC). The ATIC was created in 1993 from a merger of the military Airmiss Commissie and the civil-aviation Burger Airmiss Commissie, which investigate "near misses" in Dutch skies. Its existence is based on an agreement between the leaders of the RLD, the Dutch air force, Dutch naval

---

[11] The RLD-LI can inspect and regulate foreign aircraft sitting at Dutch airports. It has, but does not exercise, the power to refuse access to Dutch airspace and airports by "risky carriers."

air forces, the LVB (Luchtverkeersbeveiliging), and Eurocontrol. Its mandate is to investigate near collisions of aircraft; it also looks into hazardous situations involving only one airplane (e.g., aerial dumping of kerosene in the vicinity of a chemical plant). The ATIC's intensive study of selected incidents (28 in 1993) results in reports that are subject to ratification by the sitting membership.

A. **Mode.** Air

B. **Mission.** The mission of the ATIC is to examine all reported incidents of "near collision" or too-close proximity of airborne aircraft. The objective is to determine whether or not a dangerous situation existed; questions of attribution of fault are not the task of the ATIC.

C. **Sources.** Any report of an incident by any party—a direct participant (e.g., the pilot of one of the aircraft), an interested observer (e.g., air traffic control), or a disinterested observer (e.g., a witness on the ground)—triggers an inquiry. Each interested party must fill out an Air Traffic Incident form. Additional information is gathered by the ATIC secretary, as needed.

D. **Processing.** The ATIC evaluates incidents selected for investigation according to three categories: unsafe situation, potentially unsafe situation, or not an unsafe situation. The ATIC can also generalize from several incidents to make more sweeping findings.

E. **Dissemination.** Each investigation results in a report, and reports are summarized in a yearly document. Some reports include recommendations, which are transmitted to the appropriate parties (e.g., air traffic control, the RLD, airports, air carriers, the RVL). All ATIC documents are publicly available, although this availability is not advertised.

8. **Nationaal Lucht-en Ruimtevaart Laboratorium (NLR).** The NLR is an independent research firm that studies aviation and space travel. Some 80 percent of its research is commissioned by national and international governments. Safety issues play an important role within the NLR's studies, not only for risk analysis but for aerodynamics and materials analysis.

A. **Mode.** Air

B. **Mission.** The NLR conducts research by contract. It carries out most of the investigations needed by the BVOI (Bureau Vooronderzoek Ongevallen Incidenten), and therefore by the RVL.

C. **Sources.** The NLR gets most if its primary data from its clients. The rest come from its own investigations and from large databases, including ADREP, FAE, and the database maintained by the NTSB ([U.S.] National Transportation Safety Board). The NLR maintains two large databases of its own: a movement database and an accident database. The movement database is fed with data from sources such as the air control organization Eurocontrol; the aviation-accident database relies on 13 different sources.

D. **Processing.** In the safety realm, the NLR develops and runs models which permit the assessment of internal and external risk of air transport accidents.

E. **Dissemination.** Each research or investigation results in a report delivered to the client. Databases are generally not disseminated.

Rail

9. Railned. Railned is one of three task organizations within the newly restructured Nederlandse Spoorwegen (NS, or Dutch Railways). It has three major activities: capacity planning, network planning, and railway safety. Although Railned is organizationally within the NS, its railway safety activity is funded by the government; this arrangement provides Railned with rail-specific expertise while freeing it from rail company control. Railned is notified of all accidents on the rail system as well as any untoward events (about 50,000 per year). The (potential) severity of the accident or event determines whether it is investigated at the regional or national level.

A. **Mode.** Rail

B. **Mission.** Railned's safety-related mission is that of safety awareness and information management with respect to the railways. As part of this mission, it investigates the causes of rail accidents, discovers patterns in untoward events that suggest safety risks, and makes safety recommendations.

C. **Sources.** Railned receives daily reports of all untoward events occurring within the Dutch rail system. It also inspects the safety of the rail infrastructure. In more serious accidents, Railned conducts its own investigations independent of other NS units. It also receives information, as appropriate, from the police, NS offices, unions, and rail workers (via a confidential call-in program).

D. **Processing.** Accident and event information have been compiled into a relational database called the Management Informatie Systeem Ongevallen (MISOS), which will eventually contain information on all accidents since 1974 (some 6,000 in total) and all untoward events since 1989 (about 300,000 in total). This database may be queried on up to 1800 keywords. The data are input electronically, and the process is becoming increasingly automated. In a proposed revision to MISOS, Railned reports would be on-line and searchable by keyword or text search. Pattern recognition research using MISOS is ongoing and has examined, for example, black spots in the rail network.

E. **Dissemination.** Railned publishes reports of all accident investigations it conducts. These reports are reviewed by the NS and interested governmental parties before being released to the public; changes can be recommended but not required. The reports are stripped of information that could identify the parties. Internal notes compiled by Railned investigators are protected from subpoena in civil or criminal law actions. A quarterly report provides statistical summaries of events and accidents.

Water

10. Directoraat-Generaal Scheepvaart en Maritieme Zaken-Scheepvaartinspectie (DGSM-SI). The DGSM-SI is a long-standing organization concerned with the safety of both inland and maritime shipping. Its major responsibilities include certifying vessels and personnel, conducting safety inspections, assuring environmental quality, and managing inland shipping. It also investigates shipping accidents and maintains a register of police reports on shipping accidents. Under a memorandum of understanding regarding port and state control of vessels, DGSM-SI can inspect foreign ships to enforce safety regulations; however, it has no jurisdiction over the registration or general maintenance standards of foreign vessels in Dutch waters.[12]

A. **Mode.** Inland waterways, sea

B. **Mission.** Safety awareness and information management with respect to all waterways.

C. **Sources.** DGSM-SI produces much of its own information, which comes especially from investigations, registrations, and inspections. It also receives, enters, and scrutinizes accident information from the police.[13] Additional information is received from other governmental sources, such as the waterway administration. For certain maritime accidents, the Maritiem Politie Team (Waterways Police Team) must, by law, conduct an investigation and forward the results to the DGSM-SI.

D. **Processing.** The DGSM-SI has developed a number of databases from the information it receives. These are increasingly kept in electronic format and available to prospective users. NEVLOG, for example, is a ship registry and NEBAG a personnel registry. Both are kept up-to-date, and an attempt has been made to include all Dutch vessels and responsible persons (captains,

---

[12] The Dutch maritime police do have this jurisdiction. DGSM-SI coordinates efforts closely with the maritime police.

[13] These are proces-verbaal records that provide information obtained by the police through direct observation or testimony by involved parties or witnesses.

pilots, etc.). Neither, however, has yet been converted to electronic form. The SI (Scheepvaart Inspectie) Ongevallen database, initiated in 1994, maintains facts on accidents; it is not, as of this writing, yet available for use outside of DGSM. Accident investigations result in a report on the most likely causes of the accident. These reports follow no general protocol, but instead a narration specific to the characteristics of each accident; about 150 of these are performed each year (25 inland, 125 maritime).

E. **Dissemination.** DGSM-SI passes accident investigation reports to both the CBR and RVS, who in turn decide which accidents require more intensive investigation. They also provide reports to AVV and other branches of V&W. Their work is generally publicly available, but evidence obtained by DGSM-SI is not admissible in legal proceedings.

11. Permanente Kontactgroep Opsporing Noordzee (PKON). Certain units of the police have the task of maintaining safety and good order in both inland and sea waters. Some of these units, in addition, write reports of accidents with a focus on criminal or legal violations as well as causality. The PKON—one such police unit—is a joint venture of the KLPD (see below), Directie Noordzee, DGSM-SI, Staatstoezicht op de Mijnen, and others, which investigates accidents and incidents within the North Sea waters.[14]

A. **Mode.** Inland waterways, sea[15]

B. **Mission.** The mission of the PKON is to trace all legal maritime cases within the Dutch Maritime Territorium or with a Dutch interest.

C. **Sources.** Sources of information for police reports are the observations of individual police officers, plus statements from the involved parties and available witnesses.

D. **Processing.** The PKON is collecting proces-verbaal (oral testimony) reports on paper but tracks the process electronically. Its records go back 10 years. It does not analyze the data it collects.

E. **Dissemination.** The collected proces-verbaal reports are sent to DGSM-SI for further processing.

12. Maritiem Simulatie Centrum Nederland (MSCN). The MSCN, which grew out of the Marine Research Institute Netherlands (MARIN), is an independent research firm that conducts research on safety for both marine and inland shipping.

---

[14] The PKON should be distinguished from the "Water Police," which is a separate maritime police team used for activities such as the storming of drug-running vessels.

[15] PKON itself is responsible only for sea accidents. Other police units (not interviewed for this report) are responsible for inland waterway accidents.

Most of its work is in support of policy, with DGSM as the most important contractor; it has a number of other public and private clients. MSCN's basic approach is simulation of proposed new safety systems.

A. **Mode.** Inland waterways, sea

B. **Mission.** To conduct research as contracted.

C. **Sources.** Data input sources come from insurers, the AVV, the coast guard, and private companies, depending on the particular project.

D. **Processing.** The MSCN uses several models, including the simulation model SIMDAS, a traffic/accident (Verkeer en Ongeluk [V&O]) model for inland waterways, and the MANS (Management Analysis of the North Sea) for sea shipping. These models assess risk, given (among other things) the type of ship, the load carried, weather conditions, and traffic intensity.

E. **Dissemination.** The product of an MSCN project is a report, delivered to the client. MSCN staff may further disseminate their findings via professional journals and conferences. Databases and simulations, being proprietary in nature, are generally not disseminated.

13. Shipping Insurers (e.g., Centraal Beheer). Sea and inland shipping insurers maintain information regarding safety as part of their management portfolio. Some larger companies maintain their own databases; smaller insurers will share information through combined organizations such as the Onderlinge Verzekerings Maatschappijen (Maritime Insurers Group). The following information is based on interviews with Centraal Beheer, which is representative of large insurers in this category.

A. **Mode.** Inland waterways, sea

B. **Mission.** The mission of this branch of insurers is to collect information to determine risk and therefore the appropriate premiums to be charged clients. Shipping insurers also have an interest in understanding the causes of accidents so that they can recommend preventative strategies to their clients, thus lowering the risk and therefore the premium.

C. **Sources.** Insurance companies obtain basic information about vessels from their clients. The data include types of goods carried, routes, and so forth. The companies also have access to proces-verbaal reports from the police.

D. **Processing.** Processing takes place in two ways. First, specific accidents are investigated. The insurance company attempts to gather information regarding the true extent of loss and the specific causes of the accident. The analysis is qualitative and done by experts. Second, databases of vessels and accidents are compiled and maintained. It is not yet clear how these databases are used to understand the cause of accidents so as to prevent them.

E. Dissemination. Dissemination of insurance information is virtually nil. The results of analyses are largely for internal purposes. Some information is disseminated to clients in the form of recommended safety prevention measures. Although safeguards regarding proprietary data and loss of possible market advantage would have to be installed, the insurers interviewed for this report generally favor sharing information if it will decrease the overall risk of transport accidents.

Road

14. Adviesdienst Verkeer en Vervoer-Afdeling Leefbaarheid (AVV-VLL). The AVV-VLL is part of the V&W and is charged with preparing standardized reports and statistical summaries of road transport accidents. It also prepares special analyses in response to requests from the ministry.

A. Mode. Road

B. Mission. The mission of the AVV-VLL is to analyze road accidents in order to understand the factors involved. Many of these analyses focus on the influence of the road environment and infrastructure (weather, time of day, road conditions, congestion, etc.).

C. Sources. The source of AVV-VLL information is police accident reports, which are received in paper form from individual regional police corps and keyed into a database.

D. Processing. The AVV-VLL maintains the Beleids Informatie Systeem voor Verkeersveiligheid (BISV-II), from which it prepares analyses.

E. Dissemination. AVV-VLL reports are public documents and are used to make policy and safety recommendations.

15. Korps Landelijke Politiediensten (KLPD). The KLPD is a special, national-level police unit charged with, among other things, managing the safety and flow of the Dutch national autoroute system. Its mandate includes preparing reports of road accidents that take place on the autoroutes. In addition, it provides the 25 regional police corps with expert, technological, and material support regarding road safety and accident reporting.[16] Generally, the police have the task of managing the scene at accidents, including ones with fatalities or serious injuries, major economic loss, or heavy traffic congestion. There is considerable variation

---

[16] The KLPD, given its specialized function, appeared to be the best single police corps to interview for this report. The discussion extended beyond the function of that corps to more general considerations of police role in road safety.

among different regions in whether or not a proces-verbaal is taken and in what form it should be used.

A. **Mode.** Road

B. **Mission.** The primary mission of the police in this context is to maintain the safety and flow of traffic. They also prepare accident proces-verbaal statements.

C. **Sources.** Observations by police officers, plus reports of involved parties and witnesses, constitute the source of information for the proces-verbaal.

D. **Processing.** Police reports are gathered without being edited.

E. **Dissemination.** Paper copies of all reports are sent to the AVV-BG (Adviesdienst Verkeer en Vervoer-Afdeling Basisgegevens). At least some police units also send reports to the Verbond van Verzekeraars (Union of Insurers). (Due to time constraints, it was not possible to discover whether the Verbond in turn distributes these reports to the involved insurers.)

16. Rijksdienst voor het Wegverkeer (RDW). The RDW is charged with maintaining the safety of road vehicles. Its primary business is the licensing of road vehicles (and motor boats). It also sets standards for and inspects garages that do periodic safety inspections of vehicles (APK), certifies (based on evidence from the manufacturer) that makes and models of vehicles licensed in the Netherlands meet safety standards, assures the adequacy of vehicle maintenance facilities, and, at the Lelystad test center, conducts its own investigations of vehicle safety.

A. **Mode.** Road, minor involvement with inland waterways, sea

B. **Mission.** The mission of the RDW is to assure the safe design and condition of transport vehicles.

C. **Sources.** The RDW draws on various sources. Information for the certification of vehicles comes from manufacturers, supplemented by investigations at the RDW test facility to test the validity of the certification. Inspection information comes from the RDW's inspection staff and from occasional examinations of APK inspection certifications. RDW staff investigate accidents involving tour busses registered in the Netherlands to ascertain whether any design fault was involved. The RDW will also draw on research organizations such as the TNO, although it does not directly contract for such research.

D. **Processing.** As an executive (active inspection) organization, the RDW does very little processing of the data available to it. It has created a database of vehicle properties, but the information is proprietary.

E. **Dissemination.** RDW reports are generally not publicly released because they contain proprietary information. Other information—for example, regarding who is certified or the extent of violation of maintenance standards—could be used if confidentiality requirements were met, but this has not yet been done.

17. Stichting Wetenschappelijk Onderzoek Verkeersveiligheid (SWOV). The SWOV is an independent foundation with the power to give solicited and unsolicited recommendations to the V&W.

A. **Mode.** Road

B. **Mission.** The mission of the SWOV is to conduct research on a contractual basis or as the result of a government subsidy. Its principal client is the V&W. It collaborates with the TNO or university researchers when special expertise is called for. It has done work under contract to the RVV.

C. **Sources.** Sources of information for SWOV research come from its clients, the V&W, the AVV-BG, the CBS, the Stichting Consument en Veiligheid's VIPORS (Verkeersincidenten en Privéongevallen Registratie Systeem) database, and others. The SWOV also maintains its own internal databases, some of which are electronic.

D. **Processing.** The SWOV conducts statistical analyses of information using standard or specialized data analysis software. The product of this processing is a research report.

E. **Dissemination.** Research reports go to the client. If the research is supported by a ministerial subsidy, then the report is made public.

18. TNO-Wegtransportmiddelen (TNO-WT). The TNO-WT is a specialist in road accident reconstruction. It investigates single accidents in depth and performs large-scale accident research. Two different units analyze the precrash and crash phases.

A. **Mode.** Road

B. **Mission.** The TNO-WT conducts investigations and research by contract. Insurance companies and legal organizations tend to contract for investigations, while more fundamental research is typically sponsored by the government, either directly or through subsidy.

C. **Sources.** The investigatory function of the TNO-WT produces its own information, but proces-verbaal police reports are used as a beginning point. Larger-scale research generally uses AVV-BG and other nonproprietary databases.

D. **Processing.** The TNO-WT conducts statistical analyses as part of its research. The product of its research is a report.

E. **Dissemination.** Research reports and investigations are provided to the client and are generally not public unless the client is a public body.

19. TNO-Technische Menskunde (TNO-TM). This division of the TNO studies road and waterway traffic behavior.

A. **Mode.** Road, inland waterway[17]

B. **Mission.** The mission of the TNO-TM is to conduct research by contract within its area of expertise. The RWS is its major client. It has done work for the RVV.

C. **Sources.** The TNO-TM does experimental research, either in the field or with laboratory simulators.

D. **Processing.** Data from experiments are subjected to statistical analysis. Findings are written up as reports.

E. **Dissemination.** Research reports and investigations are provided to the client and are generally not public unless the client is a public body.

20. TNO-Preventie & Gezondheid (TNO-P&G). The TNO-P&G does research under contract on prevention and health; some of this work is on road traffic.

A. **Mode.** Road

B. **Mission.** The mission of the TNO-P&G is to conduct research within its area of expertise.

C. **Sources.** Base data are provided to the TNO-P&G by contractors. Experimental data from its own research efforts are added.

D. **Processing.** Data from experiments and studies are subjected to statistical analysis. Findings are written up as reports.

E. **Dissemination.** Research reports and investigations are provided to the client and are generally not public unless the client is a public body.

21. Automobile Insurers (e.g., Nationale Nederlanden). Automobile insurers have an interest in reducing the frequency and consequences of automobile accidents because such would allow them to lower premiums and therefore have more satisfied customers. Even when such increases in safety are not possible, insurers need to know the risks of accidents so that they can set appropriate premiums. Therefore, insurance companies investigate automobile accidents and commission or conduct research on accidents. The person responsible for technical accident investigation at a representative automobile insurance company, Nationale Nederlanden, was interviewed for this report. The company's 7 percent market share makes it the second largest Dutch automobile underwriter.

A. **Mode.** Road

---

[17] Although the TNO-TM studies two modalities, only a representative of the road traffic behavior unit was interviewed for this report.

B. **Mission.** The mission of the technical accident investigation department of an insurance company is to review accidents and to investigate selected ones to determine what (and who) caused the accident. Of about 300 accidents brought to the department annually, about one-third are fully investigated.

C. **Sources.** Insurance investigators obtain information from their clients, from the opposing parties, and from police reports, if they exist. The Verbond van Verzekeraars office in Zoetermeer acts as a clearinghouse for police reports. In addition, investigators make site visits and question witnesses.

D. **Processing.** The purpose of an insurance investigation is to recreate as closely as possible the situation that resulted in the accident, attempting to determine locations, speeds, and directions. Little information is kept on electronic databases, although sometimes information will be fed into specific programs (e.g., EDSMAC, CRASH) to better understand individual accidents.

E. **Dissemination.** Each investigation results in a short report that is attached to the case dossier. There is some exchange of information between insurers, and between research organizations (e.g., the SWOV) and insurers, with regard to specific projects. Otherwise, there is no further dissemination. In principle, given the appropriate modification of data to protect confidentiality and proprietary information, insurance information could inform transport safety boards.

Multimodal

22. Adviesdienst Verkeer en Vervoer-Afdeling Basisgegevens (AVV-BG). This branch of the AVV is responsible for assembling all information regarding road and water accidents within the Netherlands. Under a common management system, separate subparts deal with "dry" and "wet" transport.

A. **Mode.** Road, inland waterways

B. **Mission.** The mission of the AVV-BG is to assemble, integrate, and disseminate information about transport.

C. **Sources.** The major source of AVV-BG information is police reports, which are received from regional and specialized corps. In addition, it receives information such as hospital data from other sources. Most of the information is received on paper and must be entered into the AVV-BG's electronic data systems.

D. **Processing.** The AVV-BG is responsible for assembling data and maintaining various databases. A new project, called Projekt Plan Registratie

Verkeersveiligheid (PPRV), will redesign the process for registering information regarding road and inland waterways.

E. **Dissemination.** Dissemination of its database to other departments of the AVV, contracting research firms such as the SWOV, regional governments, and the national government is the basic task of the AVV-BG. Depending on the recipient, the information can be in the form of published summary reports or the electronically stored files prepared by the AVV-BG. Paper documents are publicly available, while electronic databases are shared on a need-to-know basis.

23. Rijksverkeersinspectie (RVI). The main task of the RVI is inspecting road, rail, and inland waterway transport to ensure safety. This mandate includes spot checks of trucks and ships to see if personnel are following regulations regarding taking breaks. The RVI is primarily a deterrent organization; inspections are supposed to induce compliance with rules and therefore fewer accidents. In addition, the RVI inspects the transport of hazardous materials in all modalities, guided here by international rules and recommendations.[18] There are 168 people in the organization, all in control tasks. In 1996, the RVI will undertake some analyses of accidents, working with the AVV and the KLPD. The RVI plans to use more preventive and less deterring means of compliance, such as educational programs, to encourage safety, and to deregulation and other mechanisms that arrive at the same safety levels as provided by the present inspection system.

A. **Mode.** Road, rail, inland waterways, any modality for hazardous materials

B. **Mission.** The mission of the RVI is to ensure compliance with transport safety regulations.

C. **Sources.** The primary source of road and inland waterways data is RVI inspection records. Rail data come from the railway companies. The RVI records the frequency and type of violations found.

D. **Processing.** The RVI does a number of summary analyses of its data, identifying frequencies of inspections and percentages of violations for different geographic areas, vehicle types, and goods transported. It is beginning to do statistical analyses of its data to identify trends related to accidents and incidents.

---

[18] The transport of hazardous materials is an area of concern in its own right, and is governed across all modalities by a variety of international rules and guidelines. These rules and guidelines affect the certification of appropriate construction and maintenance of vehicles, vessels, and equipment transporting hazardous materials; requirements for the packaging and containment of cargo; handling procedures; and crew qualification. Monitoring is done via a regime of "notified bodies" working through intermediate classification companies such as Bureau Veritas, Germanischer Lloyd, or Lloyds Register. Safety during the transport of hazardous materials is linked to more general international quality assurance developments for all phases of contact with hazardous materials.

E. **Dissemination.** The RVI publishes an annual report summarizing its activities. In principle, the RVI database could be public if confidentiality were maintained; it has not yet been used for safety research or policy formulation.

24. **Commissie Transport Gevaarlijke Goederen (CTGG).** The CTGG is an organization of businesses involved with the transport of hazardous materials, and is largely concerned with being able to analyze the risk associated with such transport. About 75 to 80 percent of the tonnage of hazardous materials transported within the Netherlands is done by member organizations of the CTGG. The organization's work includes data collection, considerations of policy matters, and seeing to the interests of the transporters.

A. **Mode.** Any mode, excluding pipeline, as long as hazardous materials are involved.[19] Particular attention is paid to situations where hazardous materials are shifted from one modality to another (e.g., from inland ship to truck).

B. **Mission.** The objective of the CTGG is to raise the assessment and regulation of risk of the transport of hazardous materials to standards within the Netherlands that have been developed for stationary facilities (e.g., chemical plants).

C. **Sources.** The CTGG obtains information on transport accidents involving hazardous materials from the transporters themselves as well as from governmental agencies having responsibilities in this area (e.g., the RVI and its DG Vervoer Gevaarlijke Stofen [Directoraat Generaal for the transportation of hazardous materials]).

D. **Processing.** The CTGG is beginning to assemble a database that will enable it to assess risks associated with the transport of hazardous materials.

E. **Dissemination.** The CTGG attempts to work closely with relevant organizations within the Netherlands as well as with corresponding organizations in other countries. Materials are publicly available, although not widely advertised. Its database is not yet ready for dissemination, but the organization has no objection to sharing it once it is better established.

25. **TNO-Industriële Veiligheid (TNO-IV).** The TNO-IV, located in Apeldoorn, is not directly concerned with transport safety but rather with industrial safety, which implies a major concern with hazardous materials. In considering the transport of hazardous materials, the TNO-IV will consider transport safety.

A. **Mode.** Any involving hazardous materials

---

[19] Although pipelines are used as a modality for the transport of hazardous materials, they are excluded from this inventory because they are not envisioned as falling under the jurisdiction of the TOR. It should be noted, however, that spillage in the transfer from pipelines to other transport modalities is a significant source of loss of containment of hazardous materials.

B. **Mission.** The mission of the TNO-IV is to research hazardous materials in order to prevent accidents.

C. **Sources.** Reports of accidents regarding hazardous materials are assembled by TNO-IV staff from various sources, including the public media, workers handling hazardous materials, and officials. Data are characterized by one to four stars, depending on their comprehensiveness and quality.

D. **Processing.** Hazardous materials accident data are assembled into a database called FACTS at the rate of about 500 accidents per year. There are in total about 12,500 accidents in the electronic database. A query program, PC FRIENDS, permits analyses using up to 100 variables.

E. **Dissemination.** TNO-IV disseminates the results of its own research in publicly available reports. Usage of the FACTS database is possible for a service fee that depends on the extent of usage.

26. University Research Groups. There are a number of university-based research groups in the Netherlands that conduct research related to transport safety. An example of such groups is the Technological University of Delft Safety Council. This council is composed of members of the faculties of Civiele Techniek, Elektrotechniek, Luchtvaart-en Ruimtevaart-techniek, Technische Bestuurskunde, Werktuigbouwkunde en Maritieme Techniek, and Wijsbegeerte en Technische Maatschappijwetenschappen.

A. **Mode.** All

B. **Mission.** The mission of the Technological University of Delft Safety Council is to conduct scientific research regarding transport safety. This research can be conducted on the initiative of the council's scientist members or in response to requests (contracts) from government or other organizations.

C. **Sources.** Sources of information depend on the particular research project and are highly varied.

D. **Processing.** Research ranges from highly quantitative model development based on extensive microlevel data to qualitative research based on macrolevel information.

E. **Dissemination.** Dissemination of research results is accomplished through publication in professional journals and books, as well as through presentations at professional meetings. For research related to safety, results may also be given to governmental bodies in the form of commissioned papers, expert testimony, or less formal discussions.

3. Information Streams

Information streams regarding transport safety are much like a river delta. Upriver, water flows in a logical reverse-branching process, with small streams flowing together to create larger ones. In a delta, though, there are various mergers and splits as water flows from one channel to another. This chapter presents a review of the information possessed by the organizations inventoried in Section 2, this time tracing a flow of major streams of information from inception through its various disseminations and uses. Again, to facilitate comparisons, a common format will be applied to each stream:

A. Mode(s) of transport examined

B. Primary source(s) of information; unit of information

C. Processing performed on data; aggregations made

D. Ultimate uses of data

   D1. Potential function for the TOR

   D2. Current use for TOR-like functions

E. Characteristics of the information

   E1. Validity of the information

   E2. Autonomy of the investigation/research

   E3. Availability in electronic form

   E4. History of continuous information

   E5. Completeness of data collection

   E6. Potential biases in data collection

Not included in this inventory are the hearings and qualitative investigations conducted by the current modal boards (the SOR, the RVS, the CBR) or the advice board, the RVV. Presumably, these investigations will be performed by the TOR or its constituent chambers. Indicated, however, is information that is external to these current boards and used by them. Investigations by the RVL are included, because this is a function that until recently was delegated to the RLD and which is substantially different from investigations by the other boards.

At the end of this inventory of information streams are other possible information streams that might be useful to the TOR and that should be investigated.

Air Modality Information Streams

1. RVL Investigations. The RVL investigates all accidents involving Dutch air carriers or airframes, or that occur within Dutch airspace or on Dutch terrain. Fortunately, these are few in number; each is thoroughly investigated.

A. Mode. Air

B. Source. An RVL team conducts the investigation, gathering data from all witnesses and parties involved. Technical information from the airframe manufacturer, maintenance information from the aircraft owner, the aircraft's recent flight history, the flight crew's history and recent experience, and data from the "black box" and voice recorder are all used.

C. Processing. Processing of data follows procedures established by international organizations. Although different accidents may generate different amounts of work, the overarching procedural guidelines are the same.

D. Uses. RVL investigations will be carried directly over to the TOR. As the guidelines for such investigations are contained in ICAO guidelines, which are part of a treaty obligation of the Netherlands, investigative practice is not likely to change with implementation of the TOR.

E. Characteristics. Because of Holland's long tradition of investigating air accidents and the expertise of RVL investigators, the validity of RVL's air accident information is high. The independence of the investigators is mandated by law and reinforced by tradition. Paper records of air accident investigations go back almost 70 years. The accident record is complete, and there are no known biases in the data-collection process. The information used in the investigations is purely a paper product; RVL studies are not yet available for analysis in electronic form.[20]

2. RLD-LI Inspections. The RLD maintains information regarding its own and other inspections of all aspects of the Dutch civil aviation infrastructure. The database includes information about Dutch carriers and airframe manufacturers, airports, and air traffic control systems.

A. Mode. Air

B. Source. The RLD-LI obtains most of its information from inspections done by the organizations it oversees. These are supplemented by spot checks done by RLD-LI inspectors to assure validity.

---

[20] Some of the information used in an RVL investigation is electronically stored by its owner, but these databases are not routinely screened by the RVL. Rather, items from those databases are supplied by request to the RVL.

C. **Processing.** Records of inspection are kept on paper. The RLD-LI scrutinizes the information to ensure its quality. Dutch information is compared to international information provided by ICAO databases. Because inspection records contain proprietary information, they are not publicly distributed.

D. **Uses.** Inspections can identify problem areas in the civil aviation system, both in terms of subsystems needing general attention and in terms of individual actors in the system who are less safe than other actors.

E. **Characteristics.** RLD-LI inspection data are generally valid. Although the inspections done by industry members are not independent, the oversight by RLD-LI and the presence of spot-checkers gives confidence in the validity of the data. This information is not available in electronic format. Data archives on aviation safety go back about 75 years. The information is comprehensive in that inspections are internationally mandated and carried out according to international standards. The oversight of the RLD-LI helps insure that the data collection is free from bias.

3. ATIC Database. This database comprises all investigated claims of too-close proximity of aircraft in Dutch airspace.

A. **Mode.** Air

B. **Source.** Beginning with a claim of a "near collision," the ATIC assembles data from standard forms filled out by the parties involved. As appropriate, information is gathered from the pilots of the aircraft, air traffic control, witnesses, and other personnel.

C. **Processing.** The ATIC closely scrutinizes all of the information to discover what caused the incident, classifying incidents into three categories of potential risk of mid-air collision. Each classification requires discussion by members of the commission and their unanimous agreement.

D. **Uses.** ATIC reports of investigations are necessary for monitoring traffic safety and identifying problem situations. Individual incidents will be investigated by the TOR following ICAO guidelines. The ATIC database over all incidents has not yet been employed for pattern recognition or statistical studies, but it could be after suitable electronic manipulation.

E. **Characteristics.** The validity of ATIC data has not been questioned, and its investigation methods are independent of partisan influence. Information is not available in electronic form, but it could be made so for a modest investment. The ATIC has only been functioning since 1993, so its database is quite recent. (Its civilian and military predecessor commissions also recorded information that might extend the base back in time to some extent.) The data collection process is as complete as the reporting of near-misses; aviation safety tradition probably means that few incidents are overlooked. By examining everybody's view of the incident and requiring a unanimous decision by the committee, ATIC avoids systematic bias.

4. OASIS (Operational Airport Safety Information System) Database. This database is scheduled to be implemented in September 1996 at Amsterdam Airport Schiphol (AAS). It is a pilot project[21] necessary to realize one of the major recommendations of the RAND/EAC safety study of Schiphol conducted in early 1993, and it is being created within the framework of the Integraal Veiligheids Management Systeem (IVMS), in which all Schiphol stakeholders participate.[22] OASIS will collect and put into a common format information about incidents at and around Schiphol, including air incidents in a catchment area 20 to 30 kilometers around the airport and all ground incidents on airport terrain.

A. **Mode.** Air

B. **Source.** Data are obtained from the participating companies, institutes, and stakeholders of the IVMS.

C. **Processing.** OASIS will link data from each of the contributing agencies into a common relational database. Inquiries to that database will be possible by type of aircraft, operator, type of incident, location of incident, weather conditions during incident, time of year, and time of day, among other variables.

D. **Uses.** The primary planned use for OASIS is incident trend analysis, investigation, and improvement measures by the participants. The principal concern regarding the potential use of OASIS by the present Bureau Vooronderzoek Ongevallen Incidenten of the RVL and its successor in the TOR is the confidential nature of OASIS data, which comes from interested parties. Public release of this information could embarrass the sources, so adequate safeguards must be built into any safety board use of OASIS.

E. **Characteristics.** The contributors to OASIS have committed themselves to providing valid, unbiased, and comprehensive data. However, the actual compilation of the database is based, as is typical in such cases, on mutual trust; data are not independent of interested parties, and there is no verification of the validity of materials. The new database is in electronic format and became operational in 1995.

---

[21] The goal of the OASIS pilot project is to evaluate whether the British Airways Safety Information System (BASIS) is usable by the Schiphol community system.

[22] These stakeholders include, among others, air traffic control (LVB), KLM and other home carriers, the Schiphol Airline Operators Committee, and the AAS. The RLD has observer status within the IVMS.

5. NLR Air Movements Database. This database tracks aircraft movements throughout Europe and is used in NLR models to predict movements in future scenarios. As the density of traffic affects risk, this database has a role in safety analyses.

A. **Mode.** Air

B. **Source.** The NLR obtains data from air control organizations such as Eurocontrol.

C. **Processing.** The NLR merges data sets, cross-checks and verifies data, and reformats for the database. The data are used for statistical analyses and entry into NLR models.

D. **Uses.** NLR research has been used by the RVL in the past, and it is anticipated that it will be used by the TOR in the future.

E. **Characteristics.** The NLR goes to considerable effort to assure the validity of its data. Most data are collected independently by different international sources. The data are in electronic format and have been collected for at least several years. The NLR strives to have as complete a database as it can. There are no apparent biases to this database.

6. NLR Air Accidents Database. This database tracks worldwide aircraft accidents and is used in NLR models to predict accident risk in the present and in future scenarios.

A. **Mode.** Air

B. **Source.** The NLR obtains data from 13 different sources, including national safety boards, international organizations, and airframe manufacturers.

C. **Processing.** The NLR merges data sets, cross-checks and verifies data, and reformats it for the database. The data are used for statistical analyses and entry into NLR models.

D. **Uses.** NLR research has been used by the RVL in the past, and it is anticipated that it will be used by the TOR in the future.

E. **Characteristics.** The NLR goes to considerable effort to assure the validity of its data. Most data are collected independently by different international sources. The data are in electronic format and have been collected for at least several years. The NLR strives to have as complete a database as it can. There are no apparent biases to this database.

Rail Modality Information Streams

7. MISOS. MISOS is the database of rail accidents and untoward events developed and maintained by Railned.

A. Mode. Rail

B. Source. Railned obtains reports of all untoward events throughout the Dutch rail system. In addition, it investigates all accidents in the system. These data are supplemented by police reports and inspections of the infrastructure.

C. Processing. MISOS is a relational database that assembles all of the information and permits text searches or searches on 1800 keywords.

D. Uses. MISOS information is used by the SOR to understand factors that influence rail safety and to identify problem situations. Individual accident reports are used by the SOR in its own investigations. Recommendations emerging from analyses of MISOS are disseminated to responsible bodies. These practices will be carried over from the SOR to the TOR.

E. Characteristics. Railned goes to great pains to ensure the validity of its data. Reports of untoward events are screened before being entered into the database. Railned accident investigations are conducted independently of other NS units, although investigations cannot strictly be termed independent because Railned belongs to the NS. As mentioned earlier, funding of the safety activity of Railned comes from the government instead of the NS in order to promote independence. The MISOS database will soon be available electronically, as will Railned accident reports. The electronic database for accidents will soon extend back to 1974; paper records exist for almost the entire century. Untoward events since 1989 are in the database. The database is as complete as possible. Systematic biases in the data collection are not apparent.

8. RVI Rail Accident Database. RVI maintains its own database of rail accidents as part of its mission to supervise rail transport.

A. Mode. Rail

B. Source. The RVI has responsibility for the NS, the Amsterdam and Rotterdam metro lines, the sneltrams between Utrecht and Nieuwegein/IJsselstein, the tramlines from Den Haag to Delft and Voorburg, and a few smaller rail lines. Information comes largely from the rail companies themselves, with Railned as the reporting organ of the NS; the other companies report information directly to the RVI.

C. Processing. The RVI maintains its database and assesses the quality of investigations; it also assures that companies react appropriately to recommendations.

D. **Uses.** The RVI acts in some ways as the executive arm of the SOR and Railned, seeing that recommendations are appropriately implemented. It also monitors the quality of the information that is passed to the SOR, and presumably will continue that function for the TOR.

E. **Characteristics.** As the bulk of RVI's information comes from Railned, its characteristics are quite similar. Information is valid, although technically not independently collected. The RVI has an electronic database of accident information that is at least 10 years old, which is as complete as possible. Systematic bias in the data collection could not be ascertained.

Water Transport Modality Information Streams

9. NEVLOG Registry of Vessels, Maintained by the DGSM-SI. NEVLOG is a register of all vessels licensed in the Netherlands. It contains historical information regarding inspections, events, vessel size, equipment, required safety systems, etc.

A. **Mode.** Inland waterways, sea

B. **Source.** Ship owners provide information for physical facts in the database; DGSM-SI generates historical information.

C. **Processing.** The DGSM-SI maintains the database. The database is used to access information about individual vessels upon request.

D. **Uses.** NEVLOG is not presently used in any form corresponding to TOR's missions. It is possible that the database will be used to detect behavior patterns or ship characteristics that are associated with increased risk of accident.

E. **Characteristics.** The NEVLOG database is valid. Independence is not at issue, because the database is a compilation of straightforward facts. It is maintained on a current basis, so the historical record only applies to currently registered ships. It is not available electronically. It is a complete collection of registered vessels and is not subject to any evident bias.

10. NEBAG Personnel (Captains, Pilots, etc.) Registry, Maintained by the DGSM-SI. NEBAG is a compilation of information on all responsible personnel licensed by Dutch authorities for water transport.

A. **Mode.** Inland waterways, sea

B. **Source.** Individual registrants provide personnel information; the DGSM-SI generates historical information.

C. **Processing.** The DGSM-SI maintains the database. The database is used to access information about individuals upon request.

D. **Uses.** NEBAG is not presently used in any form corresponding to TOR's missions. It is possible that the database will be used to detect patterns of personnel behavior or characteristics that are associated with increased risk of accidents.

E. **Characteristics.** The NEBAG database is valid. Independence is not at issue, because the database is a compilation of straightforward facts. It is maintained on a current basis, so the historical record only applies to currently registered responsible personnel. It is not available electronically. It is a complete collection of registered personnel and is not subject to any evident bias.

11. ORS (Ongevallen Registratie Systeem), the SI Ongevallen Database, and ONOVIS. These three databases cover water transport (both inland and sea) accidents and form the basis for most water modality accident investigations. The ORS is maintained by the AVV-BG, the SI Ongevallen Database is maintained by the DGSM-SI, and ONOVIS is a joint product of the two organizations.

A. **Mode.** Inland waterways, sea

B. **Source.** All of these databases are based largely on proces-verbaal reports that are completed by the police, especially the PKON. They also include reports filed by the water administration of the RWS and municipal harbor authorities. The police send these reports to the AVV-BG and the DGSM-SI.

C. **Processing.** The AVV-BG acts as a clearinghouse for accident reports. It accumulates paper copies of the reports, enters them into an electronic database, prepares summary statistics, and sends reports of these summaries to responsible jurisdictions. The DGSM-II also receives the individual reports, and conducts investigations on about 150 of the accidents (25 inland waterways, 125 sea). These accident reports are sent to the CBR or the RVS, as appropriate. The AVV-BG and the DGSM-SI are in the process of constructing ONOVIS, an electronic relational database of water transport accidents that combines the ORS and the SI Ongevallen databases. It will be ready for use in early 1996.

D. **Uses.** The reports of individual accidents are used by organizations that will be subsumed under the TOR. ONOVIS, when finished, could be used in studies of factors creating unsafe situations.

E. **Characteristics.** The information in these databases is generally valid. The independence of the proces-verbaal data-gathering process, which is at the base of both databases, is not questioned. AVV-BG information is presently available in electronic form, dating back to 1986. DGSM-SI information has a shorter electronic history, going back to only 1994; the paper archive of water transport accidents goes well back into this century. Neither database is complete because police do not investigate or report all accidents; the extent of comprehensiveness is not known. The summary statistics and part of the investigation reports might be subject to bias because police objectives in investigation differ from the goals of accident-causality investigation groups; DGSM-SI's investigations are considered free from bias.

12. MSCN Models. The MSCN collects data from various sources and builds models that predict risks of accident at sea (MANS) and in inland shipping (V&O, SIMDAS).

A. **Mode.** Inland waterways, sea

B. **Source.** The MSCN obtains data on traffic frequency and accidents from various sources, including the AVV, the coast guard, and Lloyds.

C. **Processing.** Data are entered into the models, resulting in estimates of accident risk and economic loss from cargo damage.

D. **Uses.** MSCN models have not been used by the CBR or the RVS, but they could be valuable to the TOR as test beds for proposed safety improvements.

E. **Characteristics.** The information used for MSCN models is generally valid; it was not possible to assess the validity of the models themselves. The research is independently performed. Data are electronically stored, but the MSCN has not to date shared its databases. The data collection varies in completeness—the water traffic frequency database is more comprehensive than the accident database, for reasons discussed earlier. Similarly, some of the data collection might be subject to bias; this is especially true because of the specter of sanction coming from RVS investigations.

13. Shipping Insurers Databases. Shipping insurers collect information to help them estimate the risk of claims. They also attempt to understand the causes of accidents so that they can recommend risk-reducing strategies to their clients.

A. **Mode.** Inland waterways, sea

B. **Source.** Insurance companies obtain information from government sources such as the AVV and the DGSM-SI, from collective insurance company registries such as Lloyds, from their own clients, and from their own investigations.

C. **Processing.** Analyses of data are primarily aimed at risk assessment. Insurance companies also conduct or (more often) contract for studies to study risk factors in accidents with a view to reducing accident frequency.

D. **Uses.** Although insurance company data is proprietary, it could be used for investigations of factors causing accidents if adequate provisions were taken to protect confidential and proprietary information. To date, there has been very little sharing of information bases between governmental investigation boards and insurance companies, but that may be to lack of communication rather than to unwillingness to cooperate.

E. **Characteristics.** Insurance information is generally valid. It is not independently obtained, but that is not of great concern (see immediately below). Insurance companies are increasingly putting such data into electronic form, and substantially sized databases should be available in the near future. As always, accident frequency is not complete. Because insurance companies have a vested interested in the information, they might be suspected of bias; however, their need for accurate risk estimates outweighs any incentive to bias data collection.

Road Modality Information Streams

14. Wegongevallen Database. The construction and maintenance of the database of road accidents in the Netherlands is a major endeavor involving the efforts of a number of governmental bodies, with the AVV-BG as the central clearinghouse.

A. **Mode.** Road

B. **Source.** The police are the major source of road accident information. The KLPD and 25 regional police corps compile reports on accidents. Paper copies of these are sent to various sources (e.g., the KLPD sends them to the Verbond van Verzekeraars), but the most important destination is the AVV-BG, which enters the data into its own electronic database system. Other information regarding road accidents comes from hospital reports.

C. **Processing.** Various institutions process road accident data in different ways. The AVV-BG obtains the data, enters it, checks for missing values, and enters a small number of keywords describing the accident (e.g., whether it occurred at an intersection). It then forwards the information to a number of destinations, including the governmental bodies in regions where accidents occurred, other AVV offices, and research organizations having a demonstrated need for the data (e.g., SWOV, TNO). The AVV-VLL conducts extensive analyses on these data, on their own initiative and upon request, and issues reports of its findings. Other research institutes also conduct analyses and merge road accident data with other data sources to help understand the origins and consequences of road accidents.

D. **Uses.** The road accident database is probably used by more organizations than any other source of transport safety information. It has been used for TOR-like functions for years and will continue to be so used.

E. **Characteristics.** The validity of the road accident database is generally accepted. Much independent investigation and research is based on the database. It is available in electronic form for investigators. The database for the AVV-BG goes back to 1987. A major problem with the accident database, despite its large size, is its incompleteness. Only a fraction (some estimate this at roughly one-half) of all accidents result in a police presence and therefore the possibility of a proces-verbaal. Only a fraction of the time (again, roughly taken at one-half) do the police actually complete the proces-verbaal. This means that only roughly one-quarter of all accidents enter the database. While these are certainly the most serious accidents and can therefore serve well in investigatory studies, there remains a "tip of the iceberg" problem for any possible population-based study. The other problem of the accident database is its potential for bias. The guidelines for proces-verbal reports of incidents are loose, leading to a lack of consistency across jurisdictions. Moreover, a number of interviewees commented on the unevenness of the quality of police reports.

15. Road Insurers Investigations. Road insurers, like water transport insurers, have a need to understand both the causes of individual accidents and more general factors influencing the frequency and severity of road accidents. They therefore conduct independent investigations and perform or contract research.

A. **Mode.** Road

B. **Source.** Insurers have extensive dossiers of road accidents. While these have been concentrated into an electronic database in some places (e.g., Quebec), this has not happened in the Netherlands; each insurance company maintains its own files, mostly in paper form. For some accidents (about 100 per year for Nationale Nederlanden), an extensive independent investigation is conducted.

C. **Processing.** The data from the dossiers of insurance companies lie in archives, processed very little once a claim has been closed. The investigations are associated with specific claims, and no use is made of them.

D. **Uses.** Insurance information is potentially very useful for understanding factors that influence the frequency and consequences of automobile accidents. To date, this information has not been used for any such purpose. As with the water transport insurers, this is not because of any active aversion to such use by any party, but rather a lack of communication regarding such use.

E. **Characteristics.** Insurance company data have not been subjected to tests of validity or independence; they would have to be carefully examined before being used in research. They are presently not available in electronic form, and a significant effort would be needed to enter them into computer databases. This effort could be shared among the insurance companies (who have an interest in computerizing their data) and among safety-conscious other supporters. Given the costs, it might be best not to try to consolidate previously collected information but instead to begin electronic data entry with the present. The completeness of insurance claims is a potential problem; only actual claims are recorded. Similarly, a bias in the data collection process towards determining what claims are legitimate must be dealt with.

16. RVI Inspections. The RVI conducts on-the-road inspections of freight carriers and chartered busses, as well as inspections of hazardous materials carriers in all modalities. These inspections are done by a staff of 168. Inspections include the condition of the vehicle and the driver. A major aspect of the inspections (and many of the citations for violations of regulations) concern whether the driver has had adequate rest time.

A. **Mode.** Road, hazardous materials

B. **Source.** RVI inspectors are the source of inspection information. In 1994, 84,538 roadside checks were carried out.

C. **Processing.** Inspection information is summarized into various categories (types of transport, site of inspection, percentages of types of violations, etc.) and published in RVI reports. The RVI has not yet done any accident analyses using these data, but it plans to undertake such work in 1996, in conjunction with the AVV and the KLPD.

D. **Uses.** Inspection information has been used in the past by safety boards to help recognize factors leading to unsafe transport. With the projected growth in electronic data registration and analytic capability, the RVI will be better able to assist in these matters in the future.

E. **Characteristics.** RVI inspectors' checks produce valid data in an independent manner. The data are stored in some electronic form and may be accessible for additional analyses. In principle, such analyses are possible, given that confidentiality issues are under control. The inspection data have been collected for many years and stored electronically for a period of time that could not be ascertained. The completeness of any inspection program is, of course, at issue. Given that any sampling system is by its nature incomplete, the question then becomes whether the sampling frame is adequate to answer questions that might be asked of the database. Because a major consequence of inspections is the issuance of citations, there is an inherent bias in the data-collection process, as delinquent transporters attempt to avoid inspection and inspectors attempt to oversample potential delinquents.

17. RDW Vehicle Roadworthiness Certification. In order for a vehicle to be sold and licensed in the Netherlands, the RDW must certify its roadworthiness. This certification is based on information about the vehicle. The RDW maintains a database of the information needed for certification.

A. **Mode.** Road

B. **Source.** Data for certification are provided by vehicle manufacturers.

C. **Processing.** The RDW examines the data to assure that the vehicle meets standards, and it stores the information in its archives.

D. **Uses.** No use outside of the RDW has been made of this information. The certification database, when merged with other information regarding the frequency of different types of vehicles' involvement in road accidents, could help recognize patterns of accident causation and harm.

E. **Characteristics.** The information is valid, even though it is not independently collected. The RDW is just completing an electronic version of this database. The information is complete for all vehicles certified to be sold or licensed in the Netherlands; earlier certification information is available only on paper. While there is a potential bias in the information in favor of licensing the vehicle, the data are probably reasonably free from systematic distortion.

18. APK and RDW Inspections. The RDW is responsible for overseeing garages that perform annual APK inspections. Both the APK information and the data from spot checks of garages could be used for road safety studies.

A. **Mode.** Road

B. **Source.** APK inspections are conducted by garages; the RDW inspects the inspectors.

C. **Processing.** It appears that there is no central handling of APK inspections. The RDW collects the results of its own inspections, but it does no further processing of this information.

D. **Uses.** These data are not presently used for road safety studies, but they present an interesting opportunity. Patterns of problems in APK inspections (types of problems, systematic problems by type of vehicle, etc.) might lead to a better understanding of factors causing accidents. Similarly, the garage-inspection data can help identify maintenance "black spots" and other potential hazards.

E. **Characteristics.** Novel uses exist for long-standing data, but the validity of the data would have to be tested. The RDW and APK-issuing garages are independent sources of information. These data do not appear to have been assembled in electronic form, and creating this database would involve a major effort by the RDW. Again, while paper versions of the data are archived, electronic entry would best begin with the present. Because APKs are required in order to use the roads in the Netherlands, the data are reasonably complete and free from bias.

19. RDW Bus Accident Investigations. The RDW has the responsibility of investigating accidents involving chartered buses licensed in the Netherlands. This extends to accidents both within and beyond national borders. Accidents involving public transport (*streek- en stadsvervoer*) are not investigated as part of this responsibility.

A. **Mode.** Road

B. **Source.** RDW investigators are the major source of information. Police reports, involved party and witness accounts, datarecorders on busses, and even experimental attempts to recreate parts of the accident at the RDW's Lelystad facility may be part of the information stream.

C. **Processing.** The processing of bus accident information is not unlike RVL air accident investigations.[23] Information about the specifics of the accident, background information about the specific vehicle involved and the type of vehicle in general, and experimental data collected for purposes of the investigation are brought together in an attempt to understand in detail the causes of the accident. Unlike the RVL, the RDW does not have strict international guidelines governing its investigational methodology. The investigation results in a report sent to the V&W. To date, there have been no analyses of multiple bus accident investigations.

D. **Uses.** Bus accident reports are used by road investigative bodies in the same way that air accident reports are used by the RVL. Were bus accident records to be brought together in a common database, pattern recognition studies would be possible.

E. **Characteristics.** RDW investigations are considered valid, independent studies. Reports and underlying data are not available in electronic form. Archive records of investigations date back many decades. The investigations cover virtually all significant chartered-bus accidents, but do not cover accidents involving public transport busses; adding this category of accident would broaden and enrich the database. Because RDW investigations could be used in a court of law, there may be incentives to conceal information from investigators, leading to some bias in the data collection procedures.

20. Verkeersincidenten en Privéongevallen Registratie Systeem (VIPORS).
VIPORS is a registration system that tracks people entering hospital emergency rooms for treatment of injuries. About 10 percent of such entries are traffic-related.

---

[23] The parallels between bus and air accidents are greater than might appear at first glance. Both types of accident are relatively rare but can result in high public awareness because one accident can result in a large number of deaths or injuries of paying passengers or bystanders. In both bus and air, the pilot/driver must be a specially licensed professional subject to inspections, and the vehicle must meet maintenance standards. In both cases, Dutch investigations are conducted for accidents occurring outside the Netherlands. A major difference between the two modes is that RVL inspections are not used in court proceedings, while RDW bus accident investigations are.

A. **Mode.** Road

B. **Source.** VIPORS is based on reports from 14 hospitals in the Netherlands, representing about 10 percent of all hospitals with emergency facilities.

C. **Processing.** The database is managed by the Stichting Consument en Veiligheid (Foundation for Consumer Safety), which obtains the information electronically from the hospitals and collects and stores it. Transport-related extracts from the database are passed on to the SWOV, which is the sole research user of the information.

D. **Uses.** SWOV studies using VIPORS have been conducted for the V&W and particularly for the AVV. These studies are relevant to TOR functions.

E. **Characteristics.** Information from the hospitals is generally considered valid. The reporting hospitals are not independent, but they generally transmit information of good quality. The database is managed entirely by computer; it is virtually paper-free. The database is quite recent, containing information only from 1994. The accident registry is far from complete, representing only 10 percent of all Dutch hospitals in the network; the percentage of all traffic-related emergency room visits that are made to these hospitals was not ascertained. The data are regarded as free from bias.

Information Streams Regarding Transport of Hazardous Materials

21. CTGG Information on Hazardous Materials. CTGG is beginning to assemble a database that will enable it to assess the risk of hazardous transport.

A. **Mode.** Hazardous materials in all modes except pipelines

B. **Source.** CTGG information comes from the transporters themselves as well as from governmental agencies with responsibilities in this area (e.g., the RVI, the DG Vervoer Gevaarlijke Stofen). Although the CTGG is a Dutch organization, the database could well include information on accidents outside the Netherlands.

C. **Processing.** The database is in the assembly stage and is not yet ready for dissemination. The goal is to have a common base of accident information that will permit analyses leading to policies and behaviors that reduce risk.

D. **Uses.** Once established, the CTGG database could be of use in understanding and mitigating factors leading to accidents involving hazardous materials.

E. **Characteristics.** Because this database is still being built, its characteristics are still largely unknown. The validity and independence of the data are yet to be determined. The data will be electronically available. It is not known how far into the past data will be gathered for entry. Comprehensiveness and freedom from bias are also yet to be determined.

22. TNO-IV FACTS Database. FACTS is a hazardous materials accident database built and maintained by the TNO-IV.

A. **Mode.** Both transport (multiple modes) and nontransport hazardous materials accidents.

B. **Source.** Hazardous materials accident data come from many different sources—including the media, those who work with hazardous materials, and officials—and are assembled into FACTS at the rate of about 500 accidents per year. There are in total about 12,500 accidents in the electronic database. Data are characterized by one to four stars, depending on their comprehensiveness and quality.

C. **Processing.** A query program, PC FRIENDS, permits analyses of accidents using up to 100 variables. Such analyses are used by the TNO-IV to produce reports for clients.

D. **Uses.** TNO-IV research using FACTS, although not used for safety investigations, is available to the TOR. Studies using FACTS could be contracted if the TOR saw the need.

E. **Characteristics.** The quality, and hence the validity, of inputs to FACTS may vary over sources; this is noted by the TNO-IV in its documentation of the database. Similarly, the independence of the data collection varies, as some sources are proprietary and others are independent. The database is electronically up-to-date and contains accident information for over 20 years. There is no attempt to provide a complete collection of all accidents involving hazardous materials; there is, however, an attempt to obtain as complete information as possible for known accidents. There are potential biases in the data, associated with varying degrees of independence in the data collection.

Information Streams Not Studied

In compiling this inventory, there was time to cover only information streams traditionally associated with transport safety. Discussed above are some alternative streams, including information produced or managed by insurance companies, public-private enterprises managing hazardous materials, manufacturers and designers of vehicles, and research institutes. Use of some of these streams is an option that the TOR might consider as it formulates its own operating practices. To complete the picture of the knowledge infrastructure, there are other streams of information that might be brought to bear. A few are touched upon in this subsection.

Occupational databases. Information about sick leaves and temporary or permanent disablement may contribute to the understanding of occupational accidents within the transport sector. In many parts of this sector—such as waterborne transport, fishery, offshore resource exploitation, towing, trucking, home deliveries (e.g., of mail, fast food), etc.—occupational injuries are related to events defined as transport accidents. The occupational databases might provide a way of concurrently validating hypotheses about accident-causing factors that are derived from accident databases.

Medical data systems. The world of medicine is become increasingly computerized, with hospital, physician, and payment databases being more and more commonly used. Linkages between these databases and other databases are already being used in some studies of accidents, such as the SWOV survey that employed the emergency center VIPORS database (see above). To date, the use of medical systems for accident research has been ad hoc; the science of accident research would benefit from a more systematic use of these data.[24]

Public emergency systems. These systems include fire fighting, emergency medical assistance, search and rescue, salvage and rescue, Wegenwacht (emergency road service), and other activities that help in accident situations. Front-line members of such groups have probably developed an expertise in accidents, and they know what situations and conditions lead to personal injury. Information maintained by these groups might be used in studies designed to help prevent or mitigate accidents.

---

[24] Such a use of medical databases would require confidentiality safeguards even more stringent than those currently in place.

4. Concluding Observations

This inventory concludes with a brief discussion of the aspects of information flow regarding transport safety that appeared in many of the interviews conducted for this report. The purpose here is not to come to any conclusions but rather to raise issues that might influence the eventual informational and organizational structure of the TOR.

Investigations versus Research

It is useful to distinguish between the terms "investigation" and "research." This is not a simple distinction. In Dutch, the same word, *onderzoek,* is used for both, and most English language dictionaries regard the terms as nearly synonymous. Both imply a study that conforms to the general scientific principles of openness, explicit method, and (at least conceptual) replicability. In the context of the TOR, investigation and research both refer to the use of empirical evidence to learn how to reduce the frequency and consequences of transport accidents.

Here, the critical distinction between the terms is whether the focus is on a single event or on multiple events. An investigation is an in-depth empirical study of a single event, looking at the available data from as many different aspects as possible, in order to understand that event as thoroughly as possible For a safety board, an investigation will typically be concerned with the causes of the event, while for an insurance company, that investigation might also be concerned with knowing the full economic consequences of the event.

A research study, on the other hand, is a multiple-event empirical study that attempts, by using analytic tools of data reduction, to sort out commonalities and differences among the events and the factors that determine such commonalities and differences.

This distinction means that an investigation is inherently data-expansionistic, while a research study is data-reductionistic. In the ideal world, when investigations provide the database for research, the two are synthesized. The ensuing research should go beyond simple summary statistics and correlations to more complex causal models.

A further synthesis can be realized by pattern recognition methods. Pattern recognition is a scientific approach that uses decision support tools to facilitate expert investigation of databases that are too small for complex statistical treatment but too coarse or too large for intense single-case investigation. This middle-level type of analysis, not yet extensively used in transport safety research, would be a useful technique in conjunction with a number of databases that are promising but also not extensively used, such as information belonging to private organizations.

For the TOR, the distinction means that the board must be clear whether it is requesting an investigation or research. Different expertise is required for each task, as are different time scales and analytic tools. Investigations are likely to be needed on an ad hoc basis in response to specific events, while research should be part of "monitoring transport safety and the factors influencing it"; research need not necessarily be attached to specific accidents investigated by the TOR. While the commonly perceived function of a safety board is the investigation of individual events, it is advisable to heed the advice of the Canadian Transportation Safety Board, which wrote that

> in its first five years of operation, the Board carried out enough studies and other analyses of significant safety issues to determine that a larger portion of its efforts should be devoted to the identification of safety deficiencies through the analysis of other than single events. (p. 2)

Research will link the TOR to the knowledge infrastructure underlying transport safety. It will connect the TOR to the network of research organizations so that relevant expertise can be called upon for research. This will in turn lead to the TOR having a voice in setting the agenda for transport safety research. While the value of this intense use of research seems natural, it is important to remember that the traditional association between research and governmental functions has not been uniformly rewarded in the Netherlands—any TOR use of research must produce visible and significant benefits or else the resources spent on the research will appear to have been wasted, and the reputation of the TOR will suffer accordingly.

The Problem of Denominators

An inherent part of safety assessment is determining the risk of accident, if not in precise numerical terms, then at least in rough verbal terms. An ongoing problem in such assessments is that, while the incidence of specific hazards (e.g., road fatalities, train derailments) may be well-known, the body of events that might have become accidents but did not is unknown.

The denominator to one question might not be the denominator to another. The ATIC, for example, provides a denominator to the numerator of midair collisions by tracking near collisions and sorting them into the categories "unsafe" and "not un-safe."[25] Using this information, it is possible to determine the risk of collision given the known proximity of aircraft. To study the effects of increasing air traffic, how-ever, the problem becomes how frequently near collisions occur as a function of traffic density patterns. This problem essentially requires using the ATIC informa-tion as the numerator and obtaining additional information for the denominator.[26]

In accident analyses, investigations can often provide information about numerators but rarely about denominators. Research is needed to reduce data from various sources into reasonable denominators. Thus, for transportation safety issues that revolve around the extent of risk incurred, research is likely to be needed.

Intended versus Real Uses of Information

Information gathered with one purpose in mind can often be successfully employed for other purposes. However, even when the data are carefully and objectively gathered, the orientation of the original purpose for gathering the data may lead to inadvertent or advertent bias once the context is changed. For the TOR, this issue arises because of the heavy dependence of all investigative and research bodies on police accident reports. There are at least three ways in which this potential conflict of interest can lead to less-than-desirable data collection and therefore incomplete or incorrect conclusions, even when the independence of the TOR has been guaranteed.

- The mission of the police is, first, to protect the public; second, to keep traffic flowing; and, only third, to collect information for the record. Thus, even in major accidents (e.g., the Bijlmermeerramp), the police may—with the best of intentions and quality of performance—hinder an investigation.

- When the police collect information, it is often to determine legal guilt or innocence. Transport safety boards do not care about such legal niceties; they instead wish to understand the causes of accidents. Thus, some relevant information may not be collected. Additionally, the focus of police investigations is on the micro levels of site, situation, and operator. This leads to a bias toward those factors and away from more meso- and macrolevel causative factors.

- Parties to accidents, concerned about police use of information, may be less-than-forthcoming with valuable data regarding accident causality. Even when independent investigators study accidents, ordinary citizens may not appreciate

---

[25] Note that the term "not unsafe" is used instead of the term "safe."

[26] Such safety-related research refers to current operational practices in transport systems and is expressed in terms of the margins which are dealt with in aviation by the "safe operating envelope," as defined for individual aircraft.

the distinction between police and other questioners and therefore withhold what they know.

The Limitations of Single-Modality Approaches

In examining organizations which limit the collection of data to only one modality, it became evident that a number of ways exist in which such a limitation can result in incomplete data.

- Data may be lost when modalities interact, whether in the course of transport (e.g., rail lines that cross roads) or in the transit from one modality to another (e.g., unloading cargo from ship to truck). In the latter instance, for example, if an event occurs on the ship or on the truck, a transport accident board will investigate it, but if the event occurs in transit, it falls under the purview of the Ministerie van Sociale Zaken, which upholds labor laws. Oversight of the danger may either "fall between the cracks" or be subject to duplicate scrutiny. This is a problem especially with regard to the transport of hazardous materials.

- Related to the point of ambiguity in oversight is the general problem of interministerial jurisdiction. The problem of transfer of materials between modalities was discussed above. Another example is oversight of pipelines, which are investigated by a safety board in all countries having a unified board. However, the mandate of the TOR, as planned, excludes pipelines, perhaps because they are not governed by the V&W. This constraint on the TOR could weaken its overall effectiveness and impede it from fully benefiting from cross-modality exchanges of ideas.

- Public transport in urban areas (e.g., trams), strongly implicated in the riskiness of road traffic, is not the clear responsibility of any current board.[27]

- Incident registration, a mature technology in the air and rail modalities (see the ATIC and MISOS databases), is not as well developed in the road and water modalities. This is not attributable solely to the greater frequency of road and water accidents and problems associated with reporting them; statistical sampling methodologies would make the impossible task of capturing all incidents unnecessary.

- The international research community bases its accident analysis and problem-identification activities on generic problems (for example, human factors, simulators, or navigational systems) derived from more than one mode. A single-modality approach does not reveal the existence of accident database systems and research findings of a generic nature.

---

[27] The most recent version of the Conceptwet (draft enabling legislation) places tram transport within the "railweg" kamer, replacing that kamer's old name of "spoorweg."

Conclusion

This inventory of Dutch information regarding transport safety covers all of the obvious information streams and touches upon some of the less-obvious ones. It represents a wealth of information that could illuminate our understanding of the causes of accidents, both in general and specifically. Much of this information is currently used, but a fair amount has not yet been tapped.

There are great differences among and within transport modalities in availability of information, comprehensiveness of data, and freedom of the data-collection process from bias. Some of these differences are inherent in the nature of the type of information sought, but others are due more to organizations' standard operating procedures. A fresh look at these practices might have beneficial results.

In compiling this inventory of information about transport safety, a number of issues relating to the informational and organizational structure of the TOR arose, including: the need to distinguish between investigation and research and to use both in synthesis, the need to detect causal patterns in accidents, the problem of incomplete denominators in analyses of risk, biases that may result when information collected for one purpose is used for another, and the inherent limitations of restricting one's view of transport safety to one modality at a time. A study of each of these issues would benefit the performance of the TOR.

A. Glossary of Acronyms

Symbol	Definition
AAS	Amsterdam Airport Schiphol
ADREP	worldwide database about aviation movements
ANWB	Algemene Nederlandse Wielrijders Bond
APK	Auto Periodieke Keuring
ATIC	Air Traffic Incident Commission
AVV	Adviesdienst Verkeer en Vervoer
AVV-BG	Adviesdienst Verkeer en Vervoer-Afdeling Basisgegevens
AVV-VVL	Adviesdienst Verkeer en Vervoer-Afdeling Leefbaarheid
BASIS	British Airways Safety Information System
BISV-II	Beleids Informatie Systeem voor Verkeersveiligheid (Versie II)
BVOI	Bureau Vooronderzoek Ongevallen Incidenten (of the RVL)
CBR	Commissie Binnenvaart Rampenwet
CBS	Centraal Bureau voor Statistiek
CRASH	Nationale Nederlanden accident computer program
CTGG	Commissie Transport Gevaarlijke Goederen
DGSM-SI	Directoraat-Generaal Scheepvaart en Maritieme Zaken-Scheepvaartinspectie
EAC	European-American Center for Policy Analysis

EDSMAC	an accident computer program used by Nationale Nederlanden
FACTS	the worldwide hazardous materials accident database managed by TNO-IV
FAE	a worldwide database about aviation accidents and movements
ICAO	International Civil Aviation Organization
ITSA	International Traffic Safety Association
IVMS	Integraal Veiligheids Management Systeem
JAA	Joint Aviation Authorities
KLM	Koninklijke Luchtvaart Maatschappij
KLPD	Korps Landelijke Politiediensten
LVB	Luchtverkeersbeveiliging
MANS	Management Analysis of the North Sea
MARIN	Marine Research Institute Netherlands
MISOS	Management Informatie Systeem Ongevallen
MSCN	Maritiem Simulatie Centrum Nederland
NEBAG	a personnel registry maintained by the DGSM-SI
NEVLOG	a ship registry database maintained by the DGSM-SI
NLR	Nationaal Lucht-en Ruimtevaart Laboratorium
NS	Nederlandse Spoorwegen
NTSB	(U.S.) National Transportation Safety Board
OASIS	Operational Airport Safety Information System
ONOVIS	a relational database of water transport accidents being constructed by the DGSM-SI and the AVV-BG
ORS	Ongevallen Registratie Systeem

PC FRIENDS	the front-end index of the FACTS database managed by the TNO-IV
PKON	Permanente Kontactgroep Opsporing Noordzee
PPRV	Projekt Plan Registratie Verkeersveiligheid
PRT	Project Realisatie Transportongevallenraad (project to implement the Transport Safety Board)
RDW	Rijksdienst voor het Wegverkeer
RLD	Rijksluchtvaartdienst
RLD-LI	Rijksluchtvaartdienst-Luchtvaartinspectie
RVI	Rijksverkeersinspectie
RVL	Raad voor de Luchtvaart
RVS	Raad voor de Scheepvaart
RVV	Raad voor de Verkeersveiligheid
RVW	Raad voor Verkeer en Waterstaat
SEPA	Technological University of Delft Faculty of Systems Engineering, Policy Analysis, and Management
SI	Scheepvaart Inspectie
SIMDAS	a simulation model for inland shipping accidents, managed by the MSCN
SOR	Spoorwegongevallenraad
SWOV	Stichting Wetenschappelijk Onderzoek Verkeersveiligheid
TNO-IV	TNO-Industriële Veiligheid
TNO-P&G	TNO-Preventie & Gezondheid
TNO-TM	TNO-Technische Menskunde
TNO-WT	TNO-Wegtransportmiddelen
TOR	Transportongevallenraad, or Transport Safety Board

V&O	Verkeer en Ongeluk
V&W	Ministerie van Verkeer en Waterstaat
VIPORS	Verkeersincidenten en Privéongevallen Registratie Systeem

B. Organizations Contacted

Date	Organization	Contact	Place of Interview
8 Nov. 1995	AVV, Afdeling Leefbaarheid	Drs. H. L. Stipdonk	Rotterdam
9 Nov. 1995	Nationale Nederlanden	Ing. N. L. Bosscha	Den Haag
13 Nov. 1995	DGSM-SI	Ir. H. G. H. Ten Hoopen Dhr. K. M. van der Velden	Rotterdam
13 Nov. 1995	AVV, Afdeling Basisgegevens	Ir. A. H. Polderman	Rotterdam
14 Nov. 1995	RDW	Ir. C. Kooman	Zoetermeer
21 Nov. 1995	AVV, Afdeling Inwinning & Verwerking	Ing. C. J. J. Vermeulen	Delft
27 Nov. 1995	Raad voor de Luchtvaart	Dhr. B. A. Groenendijk Dhr. F. J. Erhart Mw. M. Boyer	Hoofddorp
27 Nov. 1995	Centraal Beheer	Dhr. M. Th. Zurhake	Apeldoorn
30 Nov. 1995	RLD-LI	Ir. H. N. Wolleswinkel Dhr. F. J. Erhart	Hoofddorp
30 Nov. 1995	RVI	Dhr. Th. C. Luijks	Den Haag
4 Dec. 1995	MSCN	Dhr. van de Tak	(Telephone)
4 Dec. 1995	TNO-WT	Dhr. Driever	(Telephone)
4 Dec. 1995	TNO-TM	Dhr. Theeuwes	(Telephone)
4 Dec. 1995	TNO-IV	Dhr. P. C. van Beek	(Telephone)
4 Dec. 1995	TNO-P&G	Dhr. Guttinger	(Telephone)
4 Dec. 1995	RVV SOR	Mr. P. J. Zeven Drs. J. H. Pongers	Den Haag
5 Dec. 1995	AVV, Afdeling Basisgegevens	Dhr. Pelen	Rotterdam
8 Dec. 1995	SWOV	Dhr. Wezeman	(Telephone)

11 Dec. 1995	Commissie Binnenvaart Rampenwet	Ir. H. L. de Beijer Ir. D. J. E. M. Touw Mr. P. P. Vreede	Rotterdam
12 Dec. 1995	KLPD	Dhr. J. Bekkers Mw. N. van Ekris-van Willigen	Driebergen
12 Dec. 1995	PKON	Dhr. C. van Dijk	IJmuiden
13 Dec. 1995	CTGG	Dhr. F. E. Keuchenius	Delft
14 Dec. 1995	ATIC	Drs. W. F. van den Heuvel Dhr. R. Schulze	Hoofddorp
15 Dec. 1995	NLR	Dhr. M. Piers	(Telephone)
15 Dec. 1995	Raad voor de Scheepvaart	Mr. D. J. Pimentel Dhr. K. M. van der Velden	Amsterdam
18 Dec. 1995	Railned	Drs. W. A. Vriesendorp Ing. J. F. E. Stuifmeel	Utrecht

Bibliography

Air Traffic Incident Commission, *Samenvattend Overzicht*, 1993.

AVIV, *Veiligheid Vervoer over de Weg Eindrapportage Inventarisatie-onderzoek*, Enschede, 1994.

Borst, A. B., *3e Periodiek Verslag Railned Spoorwegveiligheid*, Utrecht: Railned, 1995.

Centraal Bureau voor de Statistiek, *Statistiek van de Verkeersongevallen op de Openbare Weg 1991*, 's-Gravenhage (The Hague), 1992.

Concept Wet op de Transportongevallenraad, memorie van toelichting, versie 29 januari 1996, unpublished manuscript.

Concept Wet op de Transportongevallenraad, versie 29 januari 1996, unpublished manuscript.

Derrike, H., and L. Driessen, *Huidige Verkeersongevallengegevens het Topje van de IJsberg?*, Rotterdam: Ministerie van Verkeer en Waterstaat, Directoraat-Generaal Rijkswaterstaat, Adviesdienst Verkeer en Vervoer, 1994.

Europese Gemeenschap, *Houdende Vaststelling van de Grondbeginselen voor het Onderzoek van Ongevallen en Incidenten in de Burgerluchtvaart*, Brussel: Publikatieblad van de Europese Gemeenschap, December 1994.

Goemans, T., and J. G. J. Joosten, *Goede Raad Is Niet Duur; Een Evaluerend Onderzoek naar het Functioneren van de Raad voor de Verkeersveiligheid en de Spoorwegongevallenraad in het Licht van Toekomstige Ontwikkelingen op het Gebied van Transportveiligheid*, Den Haag: KPMG Klynveld Management Consultants, 1993.

Hillestad, R., K. Solomon, B. Chow, J. P. Kahan, B. Hoffman, S. Brady, J. A. Stoop, J. Hodges, H. Kloosterhuis, G. Stiles, E. J. Frinking, and M. Carillo, *Airport Growth and Safety: A Study of the External Risks of Schiphol Airport and Possible Safety Enhancement Measures*. Santa Monica, Calif.: RAND, MR-288-EAC/VW, 1993.

International Civil Aviation Organization, *Aircraft Accident and Incident Investigation*, 8th ed., Montreal, July 1994.

Kroes, J. L. de, and J. A. Stoop, eds., *1st World Congress on Safety of Transportation 26-27 November 1993 Proceedings*, Delft: Delft University Press, 1993.

Ministerie van Sociale Zaken en Werkgelegenheid, Directie Arbeidsomstandigheden, *De COMAH-richtlijn en het Major Hazardbeleid van SZW; een Nieuwe Inzet van Beleid*, 3 oktober 1995.

Ministerie van Verkeer en Waterstaat, Directoraat-Generaal Rijkswaterstaat, Adviesdienst Verkeer en Vervoer, *Gegevens: De Basis voor Beleid*, 's-Gravenhage, no date.

Ministerie van Verkeer en Waterstaat, *Beleidseffectmeting Verkeer en Vervoer Beleidseffectrapportage Verkeersveiligheid*, 's-Gravenhage, no date.

Ministerie van Verkeer en Waterstaat, Directoraat-Generaal Rijkswaterstaat, Adviesdienst Verkeer en Vervoer, *Handleiding Handhaving*, Apeldoorn, no date.

Ministerie van Verkeer en Waterstaat, Directoraat-Generaal Rijkswaterstaat, Adviesdienst Verkeer en Vervoer, *Verkeersongevallen Rijkswegennet 1986-1992*, Rotterdam, no date.

Ministerie van Verkeer en Waterstaat, Directoraat-Generaal Rijkswaterstaat, Adviesdienst Verkeer en Vervoer, *Voorkomen Blijft Beter . . . Mogelijkheden voor een Verkeersveilige Ruimtelijk Ordening*, Rotterdam, 1995.

Ministerie van Verkeer en Waterstaat, Directoraat-Generaal Rijkswaterstaat, Dienst Verkeersongevallenregistratie, *VOR-Bulletin Periode 1990 t/m 1992*, 's-Gravenhage, 1993.

Ministerie van Verkeer en Waterstaat, Directoraat-Generaal voor het Vervoer, *Rijksverkeersinspectie Jaarverslag 1994*, Zaandam, 1994.

Ministerie van Verkeer en Waterstaat, Directoraat-Generaal Rijkswaterstaat, Adviesdienst Verkeer en Vervoer, *Kerninformatie Scheepsongevallen Verslagjaar 1990*, Rotterdam, 1994.

Raad voor de Verkeersveiligheid, *"Ongevallen en Oorzaken" Advies*, 's-Gravenhage, 1991.

Raad voor de Verkeersveiligheid, *Dutch Road Safety Council Triennial Report 1991-1993*, 's-Gravenhage, 1994.

Raad voor de Verkeersveiligheid, Spoorwegongevallenraad, *"Veiligheid op het Spoor,"* 's-Gravenhage, 1992.

Raad voor de Verkeersveiligheid, *Werkprogramma 1995-1997*, 's-Gravenhage, 1995.

Siebrand, S., *Veiligheid Vervoer over de Weg*, Rotterdam: VEVOWEG Projectplan, 1994.

Spoorwegongevallenraad, *Verslag Periode 1 Januari 1992 - 30 Juni 1994*, 's-Gravenhage, 1994.

Staatsblad van het Koninkrijk der Nederlanden, *Wet van 18 Juni 1992, Houdende Regels met Betrekking tot het Onderzoek naar Ongevallen met Burgerluchtvaartuigen (Luchtvaartongevallenwet)*, No. 705, 's-Gravenhage, 1992.

Stoop, J. A., J. L. de Kroes, and A. R. A. van der Horst, eds., *Safety of Transportation*, Vol. 19, No. 2-3, June 1995, pp. 81-319.

Tamminga, R., *Informatiebeleidsplan 1996-2000*, Railned Spoorwegveiligheid, 1995.

Transportation Safety Board of Canada, *TSB Occurrence Classification Policy*, Hull, Québec, no date.

Tweede Kamer der Staten-Generaal Vergaderjaar 1994-1995, 23674, *Instelling van een Raad voor de Transportveiligheid*, 's-Gravenhage, 1995.

VEVOWEG Projectgroep, Veiligheid Vervoer over de Weg, *Programma van Eisen*, Rotterdam, 1994.

Wittink, R. D., and G. C. Ederveen, *De Verkeersonveiligheid op Openbare Spoorwegovergangen; Een Verkennende Literatuurstudie*, Leidschendam: Stichting Wetenschappelijk Onderzoek Verkeersveiligheid SWOV, 1985.

Wouters, P. I. J., *De Verkeersonveiligheid van het Wegtransport: Schaalvergroting in de Toekomst?*, Leidschendam: Stichting Wetenschappelijk Onderzoek Verkeersveiligheid SWOV, 1992.